# The Gateway to the Hills

## Rapid City and the Central Black Hills

SOUTH DAKOTA
HISTORICAL SOCIETY
PRESS
*Pierre*

Black Hills History Tours

# The Gateway to the Hills

## Rapid City and the Central Black Hills

DAVID A. WOLFF

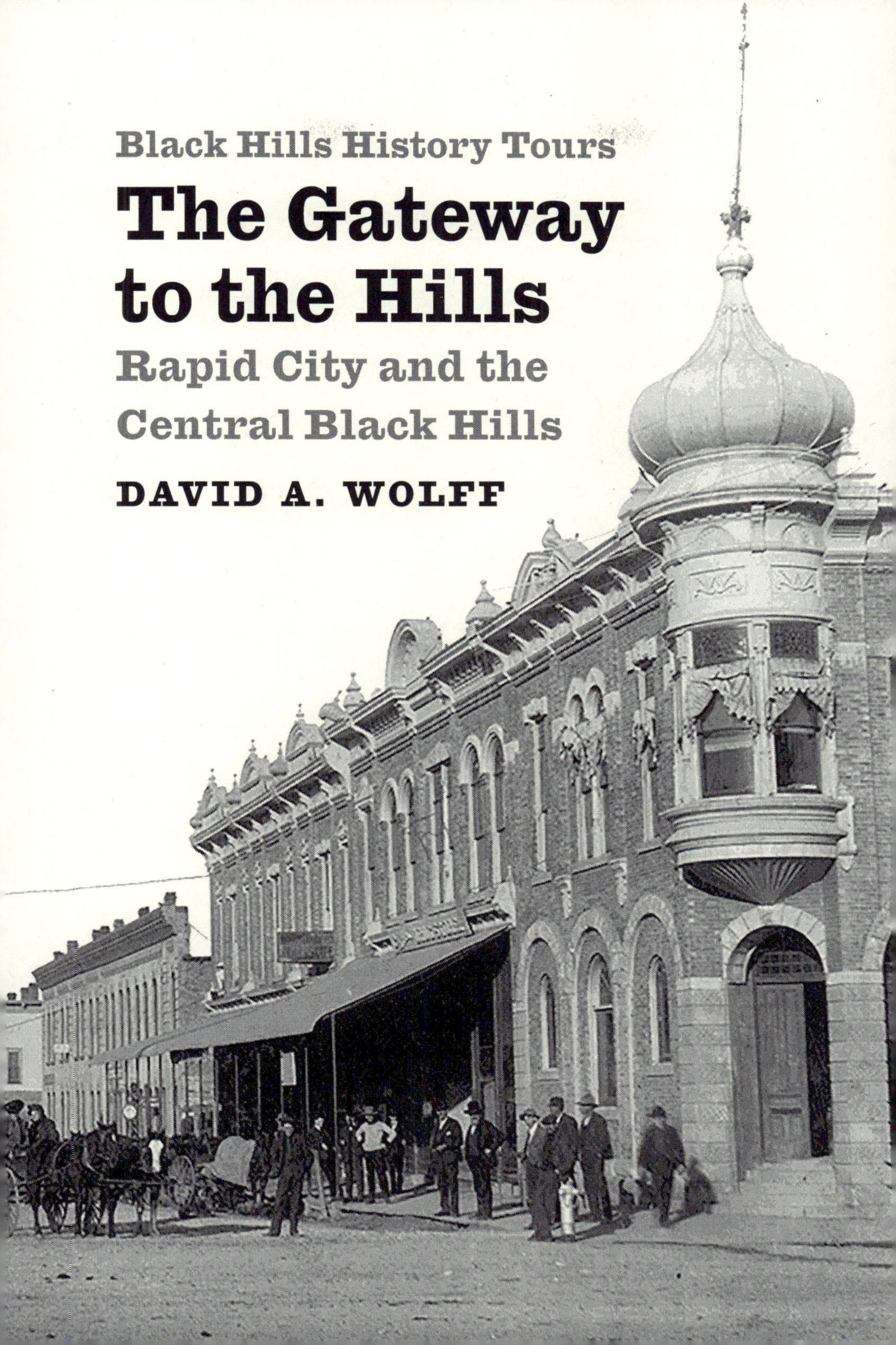

*The Gateway to the Hills* is Volume 2 in the Black Hills History Tours Series


This publication is funded, in part, by the City of Deadwood and the Deadwood Historic Preservation Commission.

Printed in the United States of America

Library of Congress Cataloging-in-Publication Data
Names: Wolff, David A. author
Title: The gateway to the hills : Rapid City and the Central Black Hills / by David A. Wolff.
Description: Pierre : South Dakota Historical Society Press, [2025] | Series: Black Hills history tours series ; volume 2 | "The Gateway to the Hills is Volume 2 in the Black Hills History Tours Series"—T.p. verso. | Includes bibliographical references and index. | Summary: "From military expeditions to gold mining boomtowns, outlandish business ventures to stunning national parks, the Black Hills teem with history as rich as their natural beauty. Inspired by field trips that he organized at Black Hills State University, David A. Wolff has distilled decades of experience exploring, researching, and teaching the history of this majestic region into accessible and informative self-guided tours. Featuring maps by the South Dakota Department of Transportation and dozens of photographs, Wolff's historical synopsis provides just the right amount of context for each site on the route, along with precise milage and directions. By tour's end, you will have completed a mini-course in Black Hills history!"—Provided by publisher.
Identifiers: LCCN 2025003151 | ISBN 9781941813584 paperback acid-free paper
Subjects: LCSH: Black Hills (S.D. and Wyo.)—History, Local | Rapid City (S.D.)—History, Local | Black Hills (S.D. and Wyo.)—Description and travel | Rapid City (S.D.)—Description and travel | Black Hills (S.D. and Wyo.)—Guidebooks | Rapid City (S.D.)—Guidebooks
Classification: LCC F657.B6 W65 2025 | DDC 917.83/904—dc23/eng/20250402
LC record available at https://lccn.loc.gov/2025003151

For EU customers with safety / GPSR concerns, contact:
Mare Nostrum Group B.V.
Mauritskade 21D, 1091 GC Amsterdam, The Netherlands
gpsr@mare-nostrum.co.uk

The paper in this book meets the guidelines for permanence and durability of the Committee on Production Guidelines for Book Longevity of the Council on Library Resources.

Please visit our website at sdhspress.com

28 27 26 25 24 1 2 3 4 5 6

# Contents



*The Gateway to the Hills* is Volume 2 in the Black Hills History Tours Series

# Introduction

# Black Hills History Tours

## The Gateway to the Hills

### RAPID CITY AND THE CENTRAL BLACK HILLS

It all began in a Black Hills history course that I taught for Black Hills State University. Because so much of what I covered happened nearby, I decided to take my students to see the locations for themselves. These field trips allowed them to connect more directly with the past than they would in a traditional lecture-based classroom. To make the field trips even more meaningful, I developed brief outlines that explained the significance of the places we visited. Each time I taught the course, I expanded the outlines. Eventually they began to resemble full-fledged history narratives. Several students encouraged me to publish the outlines as tour guides. With their support in mind, I presented these guides to the South Dakota Historical Society Press, and they saw the value in publishing them.

While I describe the guides as resembling "full-fledged history narratives," they certainly don't resemble traditional history books. Most history texts are organized either chronologically or topically, but the tours examine history based on location. Because of this format, some topics come up repeatedly as the tour goes from one place to another, and that can be a drawback. To learn more about one topic, such as the Custer Expedition, the reader will need to find entries that are scattered throughout the guide. Fortunately, the index makes that a lot easier. There are, however, advantages to this type of organization. One is that it highlights the importance of "place" in history, and another is that it reveals the "layers of history." In other words, a succession of events often took place at each location.

## Organization

The Tour in your hands is the second of six tours that will hopefully be released over the next few years: this one, starting in Rapid City; a Gold Rush Tour that starts in Custer; a Northern Hills Tour that starts in Lead and emphasizes locations related to the Homestake Mine; a Southern Hills Tour that also starts in Rapid City; and a Deadwood–Lead–Spearfish Tour and a Belle Fourche River–Wyoming Tour that both start in Spearfish. Two of the tours are organized with a theme in mind: the Gold Rush Tour and the Homestake–Northern Hills Tour. These tours focus on locations generally related to the theme, but they also discuss historic sites encountered along the way. The other tours visit locations based on their proximity to one another. Sometimes the routes of the theme- and location-based tours overlap, and when that happens, both tours will include a discussion of the duplicated sites. This is done so that nothing of interest is missed along a tour's route. Another result of having multiple tours is that the details of some of the Black Hills' most famous landmarks are discussed in only one tour. For instance, Mount Rushmore's full story is told in this, the Rapid City and Central Black Hills Tour, but it is also briefly mentioned in the Gold Rush Tour. Finally, many Black Hills towns have excellent museums, but these are only briefly mentioned. I encourage you to explore these museums on your own.

## Topics

The topics included in each guide were determined by what happened at the locations the tours visit. As I mentioned, sometimes there is overlap between tours, and the same topics and locations appear in multiple tours. I did not want information to be missed if the user chose to do one tour but not another.

## Using the Guide

The tour can be done in one day, but how long it takes depends on the user. The route is divided into sections, with each section ending at a Recommended Stop. These breaks are meant to provide an opportunity to read the narrative for that location and for what lies ahead, but they can be used as bookmarks to leave the tour and return to it later. Approximate mileages are provided for each section. The mileages were checked for accuracy, but there will undoubtedly be variation.

When traveling, visitors will find that sites come and go quickly and that traffic can be heavy, especially in towns. Consequently, it is recommended that the tour narrative be read in advance. At some of the busiest locations, such as downtown Rapid City, you should stop and visit the area on foot. Those who follow the tour guide do so at their own risk. The author and the publisher, the South Dakota Historical Society Press, bear no responsibility for any accidents and mishaps.

The tours follow roadways owned and maintained by government agencies, either federal, state, county, or city. Please adhere to the public rights-of-way and be respectful of private property. Courtesy of the South Dakota Department of Transportation (SDDOT), maps of the route are provided for each section, as well as a general map for each tour. Road construction and road closures can and will affect the tours. For instance, SDDOT anticipates closing parts of US 385 through the central Black Hills beginning in 2024. If closures are encountered, you will need to improvise.

*The Gateway to the Hills* is accurate as written in the summer of 2024. It begins in Rapid City and then moves into the Black Hills, exploring Keystone, Mount Rushmore, Custer, Hill City, Sheridan Lake, and Pactola Dam, before returning to Rapid City. Several historic and scenic points are mentioned along the way. The tour is broken into ten parts with nine Recommended Stops.

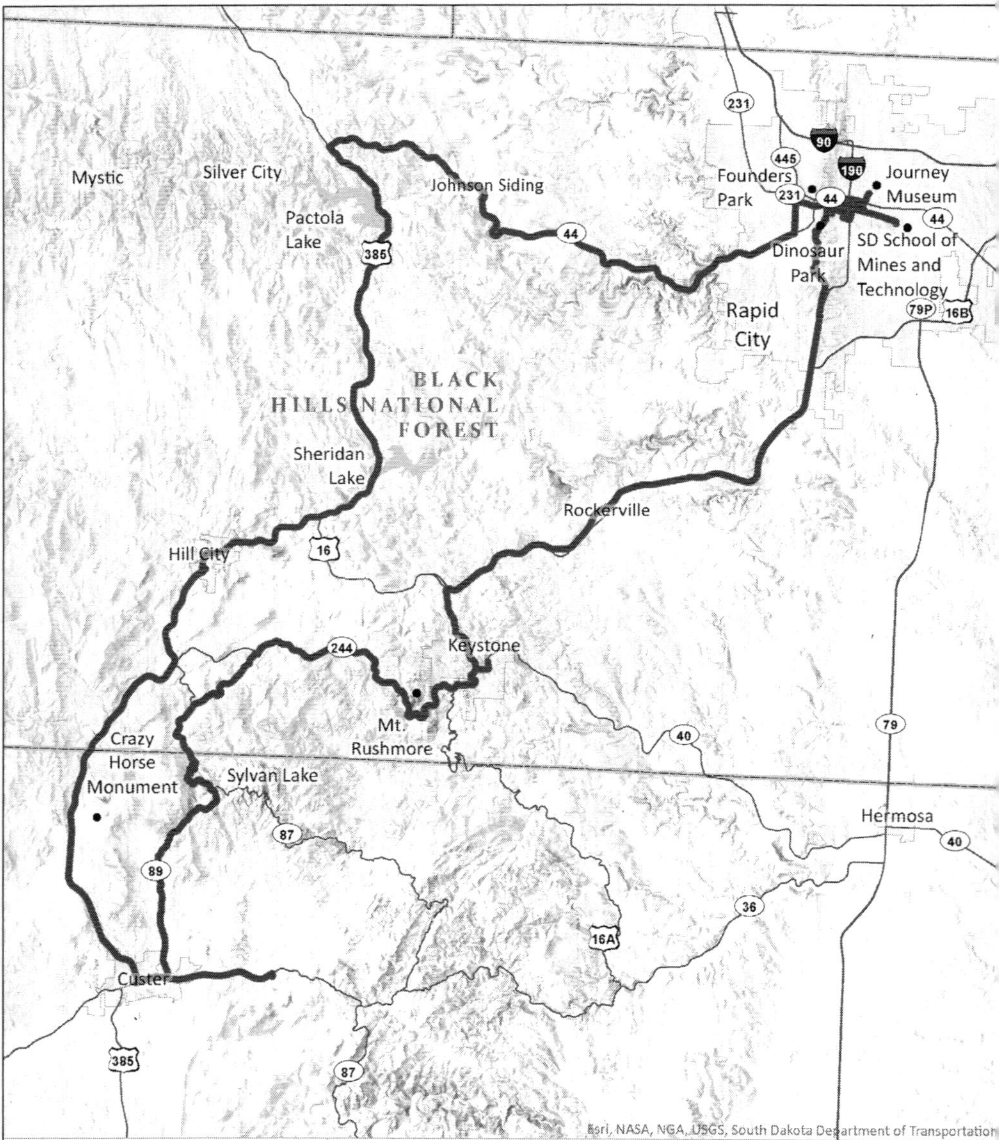


# THE GATEWAY TO THE HILLS

## Tour Overview

**The Gateway to the Hills Tour starts at Rapid City's Journey Museum, 222 New York Street.**

The museum sits two blocks east of 5th Street, not far from the Rapid City Civic Center. A visit to the museum is recommended.

**Introduction to the Journey Museum:** The Journey Museum's displays are dedicated to paleontology, geology, archaeology, American Indians, and pioneers. Several agencies came together in 1997 to make the museum a reality. The South Dakota School of Mines Museum of Geology works with the paleontology and geology sections; the South Dakota State Historical Society curates the archaeology area; the Indian Arts and Crafts Board's Sioux Indian Museum has its collection on display; and the Black Hills Historical Society (formerly known as the Minnilusa Historical Association) highlights the pioneer experience.

**Pap Madison cabin:** The oldest known structure in Rapid City is on the museum's grounds. Rufus Madison built the cabin at the corner of 5th and Rapid Streets, near the center of Rapid City's original survey, in 1876. Madison lived in it for only a short time before moving to a ranch. Town founder John Brennan then used the structure as a barn, causing it to deteriorate. Wishing to save the cabin, Brennan's wife eventually donated it to the city. In 1926, local officials moved it to Halley Park, just west of downtown. They also replaced deteriorating logs and added a fireplace. For a time, the cabin served as the town's first museum. To make it more accessible, it was moved to the Journey Museum in 2012. A stone marker next to the building has a verse written in its honor by Richard B. Hughes, an early editor of the *Rapid City Journal.*

**Alice Gossage Monument:** The concrete column next to the Pap Madison cabin honors newspaper publisher and activist Alice Gossage. Her husband, Joseph, co-founded the *Rapid City Journal* in 1878. When he became ill in the late 1880s and eventually died, she took on the management and editorship of the paper. In addition, she worked to gather and distribute clothing and toys to the needy. After Gossage died in 1929, tributes called her the "mother of Rapid City." The

Alice Gossage, "the mother of Rapid City." *Black Hills National Forest Historical Collection*

Fortnightly Club, a women's organization dedicated to learning, greatly admired Gossage and decided to build a memorial to her in 1935. At that time, the Works Progress Administration (WPA, a Roosevelt New Deal program that provided manual labor jobs) was constructing Skyline Drive above Rapid City, and the club wanted to place the monument at the highest point on the road. After three years of fundraising, which included WPA support, in June 1938 the members dedicated a memorial that featured a five-foot-tall concrete pillar, a sundial, a bronze plaque, and several benches. Unfortunately, it quickly became an afterthought, and when television stations began acquiring property for their towers on Skyline Drive, one took over the memorial's location in 1957. The concrete pillar and benches were pushed aside, but to preserve Gossage's memory the plaque and sundial were relocated, first to the stone pillar in Halley Park, then to the Journey Museum grounds in 2025.

**Ellsworth Air Force Base:** About seven miles east of the Journey Museum, northeast of Box Elder, is Ellsworth Air Force Base (AFB). Established during World War II, this military facility dramatically influenced Rapid City's development. Changes in the city's population partly reflect the base's impact: around 14,000 people lived in Rapid City in 1940, but the population nearly doubled to 25,000 by 1950.

The U.S. Army Air Corps (the forerunner of the Army Air Forces and later the U.S. Air Force) established the Rapid City Army Air Base in early 1942 as a training site for B-17 Flying Fortress crews bound for

Europe. The nearby southern Badlands, devoid of people and air traffic, provided a suitable training ground for the crews to safely practice bombing runs. Out of the four hundred crews that trained at the base from 1942 to 1945, eight were involved in accidents, killing a total of fifty military personnel, but no civilians. A few non-fatal mishaps also occurred. In one instance, a bomber crew defied orders and flew too low over downtown Rapid City. Its trailing antenna knocked the sign off the roof of the Hotel Alex Johnson.

The base was put on standby in July 1945 following Nazi Germany's surrender but was soon reactivated as a permanent facility in response to the burgeoning Cold War. In 1953, President Dwight D. Eisenhower rededicated it in honor of Brigadier General Richard E. Ellsworth, who died in a crash off the coast of Newfoundland during a training mission. The base has had a variety of missions since 1945, including serving B-36 Peacemakers, the biggest bombers ever built. To accommodate the massive aircraft at Ellsworth, the Air Force constructed one of the largest hangars in the world. The B-36s were eventually replaced by B-52 Stratofortresses, an air-tanker command, and a missile wing. Today Ellsworth primarily serves B-1B bombers.

**A Brief History of Rapid City:** Determined to find an easier way to make money, in February 1876 John Brennan, Sam Scott, and several

Ellsworth Air Force Base, undated. *Black Hills National Forest Historical Collection*

other miners abandoned their placer claims in Palmer Gulch. Brennan, having recently lived in Denver, where he had witnessed how the city prospered by supplying the Colorado gold rush, hoped to duplicate that success for the Black Hills. He and his associates followed Rapid Creek out onto the plains. While camped under Point of Rocks, near today's Founders Park, they dreamed of a new Denver spreading out before them. With a pocket compass, Scott laid out a one-square-mile townsite, which the men named Rapid City. Scott then divided it into ten blocks, bounded by West and East Boulevards and North and South Streets and centered at the intersection of 5th and Rapid Streets. Scott's compass was aligned with magnetic north, so the original part of the town sits at a slight angle from the later additions that were surveyed from true north. With Rapid City established, the founders worked to ensure its success. They organized a townsite company, chose five trustees to manage its affairs, built a few log cabins at the center of town, and opened the first businesses. In the meantime, Brennan and four other men headed east to open a trail to Fort Pierre, hoping to attract settlers. They had quick success; two parties of one hundred men each soon followed them to the Black Hills.

Their plans, however, hit a snag. The 1868 Fort Laramie Treaty had set aside the

John Brennan, the founder of Rapid City (wearing black hat). This photo would have been taken when Brennan was U.S. Indian Agent at Pine Ridge Indian Reservation, ca. 1910s. *South Dakota State Historical Society*

Sioux Indian Reservation (later known as the Great Sioux Reservation), including the Black Hills, as Lakota territory. The U.S. Army may have abandoned its efforts to keep prospectors out of the Black Hills, but Lakota warriors had not, and the new town was a convenient target. In July and August 1876, Lakotas reportedly killed nine men en route to Rapid City, while another four died close to town. The two hundred settlers at Rapid City fled in fear, except for eighteen men and one woman who stayed and built a two-story blockhouse at the intersection of 5th and Rapid Streets. It provided them a safe environment for the rest of the summer.

As the danger subsided, people returned, and businesses reopened. Most importantly, travelers bound for Deadwood began passing through Rapid City. Freight wagons and stagecoaches soon became common sights on the city's streets. Teams enjoyed the forage along Rapid Creek, earning the town the nickname "Hay Camp." The traffic attracted outlaws, especially horse thieves. In response, Rapid City residents formed a posse. In June 1877 they hanged three suspected horse thieves on a hill on the western edge of town. Since then, the location has been known as Hangman's Hill.

Rapid City got a small economic boost when it became the seat of Pennington County later that year, but it sat too far from the major gold fields to grow much beyond its camp beginnings. The census taker found only 335 people there in 1880, making it only slightly larger than Rockerville and Rochford, two other Pennington County towns. By contrast, the boomtown of Deadwood had nearly 3,800 people by 1880. John Brennan still envisioned his town as a transportation and service center, and he knew that would require a railroad. Although it took ten years, the Fremont, Elkhorn & Missouri Valley finally arrived in 1886. The town's residents celebrated, for good reason, as the first passenger train pulled into the station in early July. The railroad made Rapid City its terminus for a year. As a result, several prominent structures went up in the mid-1880s, and the census taker counted over 2,100 people in 1890.

The good times did not last. As gold mining became more focused in the northern Black Hills, and more railroads built into the region, Rapid City's importance diminished. Its population dipped to about 1,350 by 1900. Hoping to reverse this trend and tie Rapid City more closely to the Black Hills' economy, city boosters invested in rail schemes and ore processing plants. The Rapid Canyon Line (RCL), also known as the Crouch Line, was probably the most ambitious of the rail projects. It took fifteen years and a large amount of local financing to finish the thirty-two-mile railroad from Rapid City to Mystic by 1906. Along with investing in the RCL, businessmen also supported the construction of a smelter on the southern edge of town. Neither project brought sustained, long-term growth. Renewed prosperity only came when the Chicago and North Western and the Chicago, Milwaukee, St. Paul and Pacific Railroads built to Rapid City in 1907. These two lines gave Rapid City more rail connections and attracted homesteaders and town builders to western South Dakota, greatly expanding Rapid City's market. The town's population tripled to more than 3,800 people by 1910, with more on the way. New enterprises opened, including a large sawmill. Auto travelers and early tourists further enhanced Rapid City's economy, finally turning it into the "Denver of the Black Hills" and the "Gateway to the Hills" that Brennan had dreamed of years before. Today, Rapid City is the second largest city in South Dakota, with a population of 74,703 people according to the 2020 Census.

## Part One

# Omaha Street and Founders Park

Route Overview: From the Journey Museum, take New York Street to the 5th Street intersection. Turn left (south) onto 5th Street. Travel south to Omaha Street. Turn right (west) onto Omaha Street and follow it to Founders Park for a Recommended Stop.

Mileage starts at the Journey Museum.

0.0 mi **Journey Museum, Rapid City. Follow New York Street to 5th Street intersection.**

0.3 mi **Junction of New York and 5th Streets.**
**Turn left (south) onto 5th Street, toward Omaha Street.**
**Move into the right lane of 5th Street.**

**Street Names:** The town founders named several of the east-west streets after major cities: Omaha, Kansas City, Chicago, St. Louis, New York, Philadelphia, and Denver.

0.5 mi **Grain elevator at the intersection of 5th and Omaha:** The Hubbard grain elevator, marking the location of an early flour mill, dominates the corner of 5th and Omaha. In 1889, a group of businessmen led by bankers R. C. Lake and James Halley organized the Rapid River Milling Company. They chose this location for its proximity to Rapid Creek, which supplied the power, and for the nearby rail connections. As the mill went up, the company diverted the creek's water by digging a 2,000-foot flume from near 8th Street to the mill. The water then returned to the creek near 2nd Street. The mill's Swan's Down flour became popular throughout the Black Hills.

After nearly forty years of operation, Rapid River Milling sold to the Tri-State Milling Company of Belle Fourche. The Quarnberg family started Tri-State Milling in 1913, offering Trisco flour as its premier product. They soon expanded across western South Dakota,

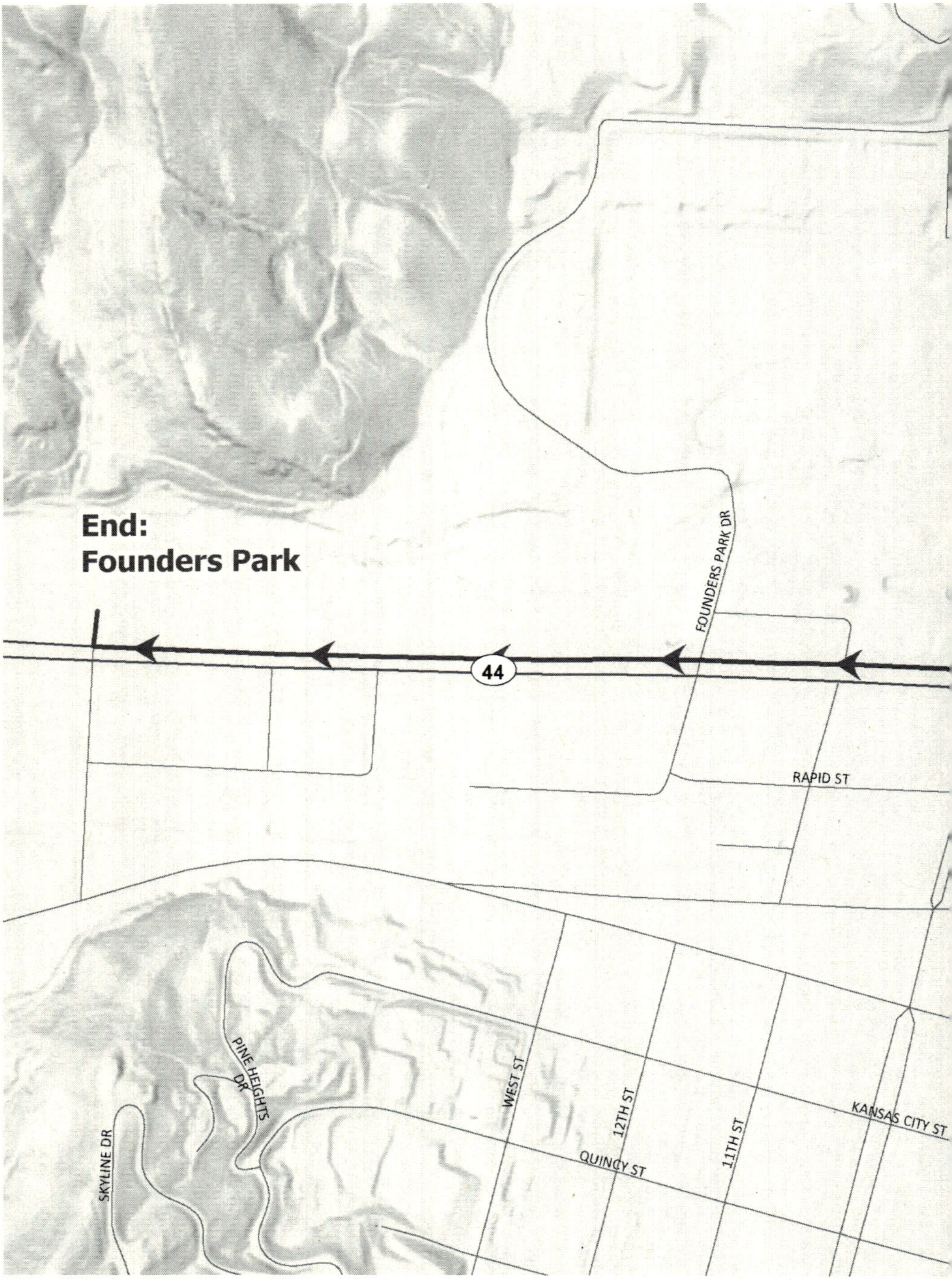
End:
Founders Park
44
FOUNDERS PARK DR
RAPID ST
PINE HEIGHTS DR
WEST ST
12TH ST
11TH ST
KANSAS CITY ST
QUINCY ST
SKYLINE DR

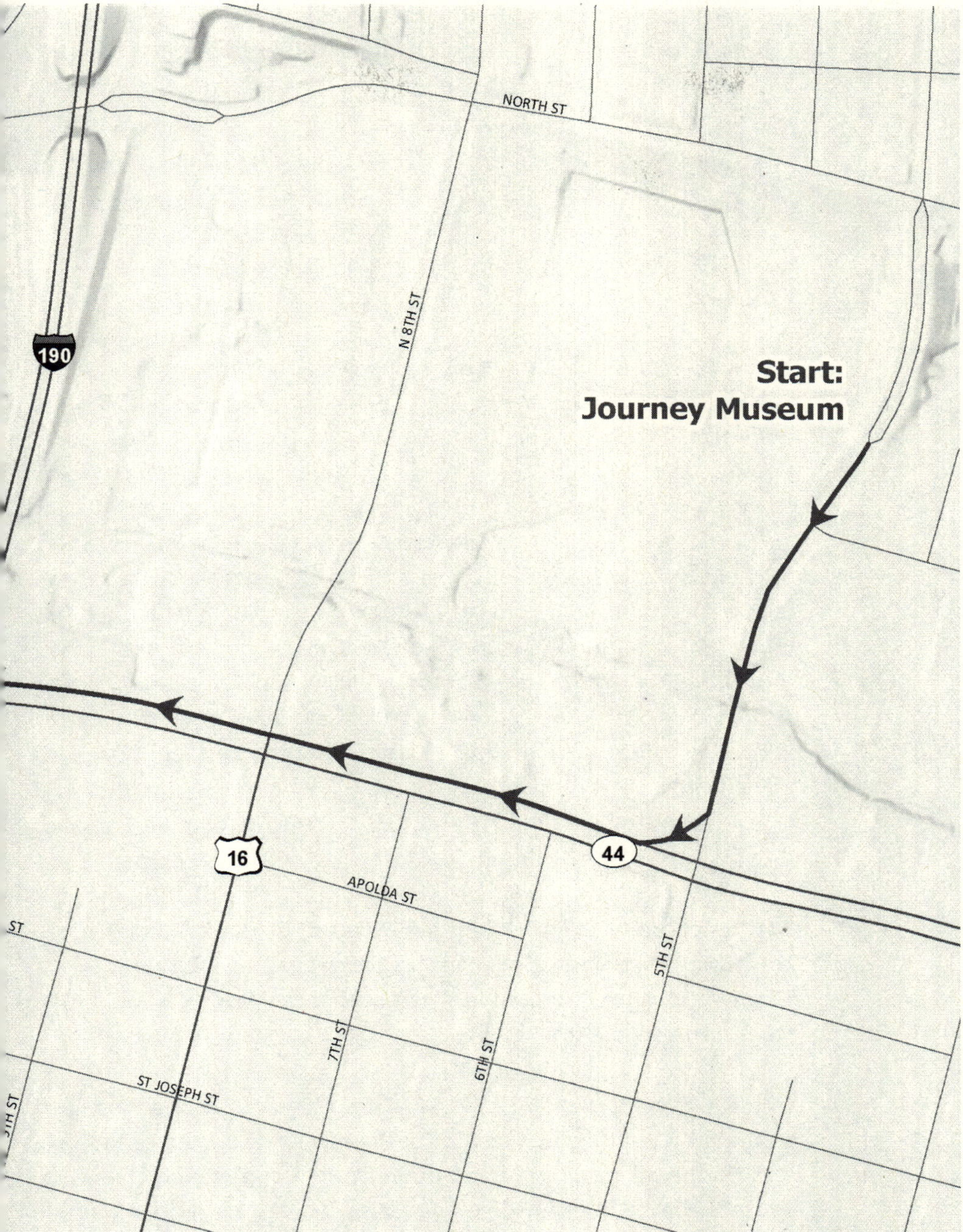
NORTH ST
N 8TH ST
190
Start:
Journey Museum
16
44
APOLDA ST
ST
5TH ST
7TH ST
6TH ST
ST JOSEPH ST
Esri, NASA, NGA, USGS, FEMA, South Dakota Department of Transportation

which included acquiring the Rapid City mill. In 1938, after operating the old plant for nearly a decade, Tri-State Milling built a new facility. The new mill was described as one of the most modern in the country, and the 110-foot elevator tower was called the "tallest building in the state." The company used the old plant to handle commercial feeds.

The Quarnbergs sold to Hubbard Milling of Mankato, Minnesota, in 1970, and Dakota Mill & Grain acquired the ten-story elevator in 2005. The complex currently hosts two agricultural entities, Hubbard Feeds and Dakota Mill & Grain.

**Aby's Feed & Seed Elevator:** A four-story grain elevator is visible one block south of the intersection of 5th and Omaha. Frank McMahon erected this elevator in 1936. A Black Hills pioneer, McMahon became known as the "baled hay man" when he opened a feed store in the Flormann Block at the corner of 6th and St. Joseph Streets in 1896. To better access rail connections, he relocated to the corner of 5th and Rapid, where he built a brick store. As he expanded into seed, hay, grain, and coal sales, he added more structures, including the four-story elevator. McMahon's son took over the business and ran it until 1961, when he leased the buildings to Bober Seed and Feed. Bober sold to Aby's Feed & Seed in 1970. The Aby company closed in 2001. The buildings sat empty for a time, but they have recently been turned into an arts center.

Businesses like Rapid River Milling and the McMahon Company provided a big boost to Rapid City's early agricultural economy.

0.5 mi **Intersection of 5th and Omaha: Turn right (west) onto Omaha Street. Travel on Omaha Street to Cross Street. Turn right onto Cross Street to Founders Park for a Recommended Stop.**

**Omaha Street environs:** Omaha Street is a major thoroughfare today, but it once sat just outside of Rapid City's main business district. In the town's early years, buildings went up along Main and St. Joseph Streets, but few appeared along Omaha. Most people worried about Omaha's proximity to Rapid Creek; in the 1883 flood many of them had witnessed Rapid Creek overflow its banks and cover

Omaha Street, while Main and St. Joseph stayed dry. Nevertheless, Omaha Street eventually attracted warehouses, small industries, and some other less reputable enterprises.

In fact, Rapid City's most notorious establishments sat in the creek basin three blocks east of 5th Street. Rapid Creek branched near 2nd Street, creating an isolated piece of land that attracted honky-tonk bars. With such famous "ladies of the night" as Black Nell and Dora DuFran reportedly opening businesses there, this "playground" became known as Coney Island. One story claims that on a stormy night in June 1907, high water washed out the bridge to the island, trapping the revelers, some of Rapid City's most influential citizens among them. As the evening grew late, a crowd of fifty angry women gathered along the creek, waiting for their errant husbands. At dawn, the water had receded enough for the men to sheepishly wade across the creek and into the arms of their wives.

When the railroads arrived, they placed their tracks along Omaha and Rapid Streets (one block south of Omaha), bringing more industrial development to the area. The Lanphere-Hinrichs Lumber Company (later to become the Warren-Lamb Lumber Company) and the Rapid City Packing Company plant opened next to the railroad tracks, near the western end of Omaha Street. The street, however, remained of secondary importance and had previously ended at 12th Street until Warren-Lamb allowed the city to extend it across the sawmill's property toward western Rapid City in 1944. Omaha's extension turned it into a major artery. By the time of the 1972 Black Hills Flood, auto dealerships and light industries sat along Omaha Street, and Rapid City's homeless population lived in shanties next to the creek. These businesses and residents felt the full force of the flood. After that disaster, Rapid City passed zoning ordinances to prevent similar activities from returning to the floodplain north of Omaha Street.

**Omaha Street Overview:** The ten-block trip from 5th Street to Founders Park passes four former railroad structures on the south as well as a city park, created after the 1972 flood, on the north. The three railroads that served Rapid City in the early twentieth century are represented by the four structures. Since they are close together, and Omaha Street is often busy, exact mileages are not provided. Some of the locations mentioned along this route are on side streets and cannot be easily viewed from Omaha. Pulling off and taking time to see the sights on foot is advisable.

**Chicago and North Western Warehouse (1932), 413 6th Street:** On 6th Street, one block south of Omaha, is a former railroad warehouse. Built in 1932, the large utilitarian structure had a railroad platform on the north and several truck docks on the east to facilitate the transfer of freight. It continues to serve as a warehouse. The brick and concrete building has Art Deco highlights.

Art Deco (short for *Arts Dècoratifs*) originated in France in the 1920s and was popular in the United States into the 1930s. Many architectural styles are revivals of earlier designs, but Art Deco, with its sleek, linear, streamlined features, sometimes embellished with geometric designs, was meant to represent a new, modern age. The Chrysler Building in New York City is a famous example of the type. Rapid City has several historic structures with Art Deco features.

0.6 mi **Milwaukee Road Passenger Station (1930), 603 Omaha Street:** According to newspaper articles, the Milwaukee Railroad built a passenger station at this location soon after it arrived in 1908. The small station contained men's and women's waiting rooms, toilets, and a baggage room. It went through several renovations over the years, including an entire reconstruction in 1930. Once the Milwaukee abandoned its line in 1980, other businesses took ownership of the building and modified it for a variety of uses, including a restaurant.

**Milwaukee Road Freight Station (1930), 655 Omaha Street:** The Milwaukee built a freight station next to its passenger station in 1908. The railroad eventually replaced it with this brick and concrete structure. Some sources call it a 1920s-era building, but the *Rapid City Journal* reported it was constructed in 1930. After the Milwaukee ended operations, it was used as a warehouse for nearly ten years, followed by a night club, a restaurant, and offices. When it was listed on the National Register of Historic Places, a state preservation of-

The Crouch Line office building, shown in a 1906 promotional piece.
*Journey Museum, Rapid City, S.Dak.*

ficial called it the "best surviving example of historic railroad properties in Rapid City."

0.7 mi **Crouch Line Warehouse and Office (1891), 321 7th Street:** On 7th Street, one block south of Omaha Street, is a three-story Italianate building dating from 1891. William T. Coad, the originator of the RCL or Crouch Line Railroad, used it as an office and warehouse. It had two large doors on the south side where freight could be transferred between the warehouse and nearby railroad cars. At one time, the railroad's passenger station sat a block west of the warehouse. The Crouch Line operated until 1947, but the company stopped using the building prior to that time. Other businesses continued to use the structure as a warehouse, but more recently it has housed a pub.

The Italianate features on the building include the tall, arched windows and decorative cornice. Italianate architecture, first popularized in Great Britain in the early nineteenth century, drew inspiration from sixteenth century Italian Renaissance architecture. Italianate buildings went up throughout the Black Hills and the West in the 1880s and 1890s, including several in downtown Rapid City. Most of them were built when the town boomed after the arrival of the Fremont, Elkhorn & Missouri Valley Railroad in 1886.

**1972 Flood Overview:** The 1972 Black Hills Flood was a defining moment in Rapid City's history. On the evening of 9 June, heavy rain fell along the eastern edge of the Black Hills. Several creeks flooded, including Bear Butte and Boxelder to the north of Rapid City and Grizzly Bear to the south. Water and debris surged along Rapid Creek and built up on Canyon Lake's earthen dam, which soon failed. More than 1,300 homes and businesses were washed away. A total of 238 people throughout the Black Hills lost their lives and thousands more were displaced. In the flood's aftermath, the city resolved to keep the floodplain clear of buildings and put in greenways, parks, and paths. Still, some developers have sought permission to build in the floodplain.

**Memorial Park:** To the north of Omaha Street is Memorial Park. The 1972 flood devastated the structures that sat in this area. To prevent future disasters and to remember those who lost their lives in the flood, the city turned the space into a greenway and built Memorial Park. Since the park's creation a Black Hills Veterans Memorial has been added to honor servicemen who have died in combat, and a statue by Dale Lamphere titled "Legacy" was commissioned to commemorate the state's centennial.

**Berlin Wall Memorial, 206 North 8th Street (Mt. Rushmore Road):** Two blocks north of Omaha Street are two sections of the Berlin Wall and several interpretative panels that explain their significance. Each four feet wide, thirteen and a half feet tall, and six inches thick, the sections were originally located between Berlin's Brandenburg Gate and Checkpoint Charlie. Despite having little direct connection to Rapid City, the wall has become a popular tourist stop since its installation in 1996.

Founder's Park, 2022. *Author photo*

1.4 mi **Intersection of Omaha and Cross Streets.**
**Turn right (north) to access Founders Park for a Recommended Stop.**

**Founders Park, 1510 West Omaha Street:** Founders Park was established near the campsite of John Brennan and his partners when they laid out Rapid City in early 1876. The park has interpretative signs and a map highlighting the area's history, including the presence of American Indians and the town's development.

**The Gap:** The area between the two mountain ridges is known as the Gap. With the hillsides offering shelter and the creek providing water, early travelers, from American Indians to Rapid City's founders, used this location as a campsite. As the town developed, the Gap became a dividing line between east and west Rapid City. Thousands of commuters travel through it daily.

**Cowboy Hill/M Hill:** The small mountain to the north of Founders Park is known as Cowboy Hill or M Hill. Local merchants purportedly named it Cowboy Hill to honor those who attended the annual cattle roundups of the 1880s. Faculty and students created the stone and concrete "M" on the hillside to advertise the South Dakota School of Mines in 1912. Students still hold an annual event to paint the letter.

**Industrial development:** Three industries important to Rapid City's early development once stood near Founders Park. The promoters of the enterprises chose this location because of its proximity to Rapid Creek and to nearby rail lines.

**Hydroelectric Plant:** One of Rapid City's earliest electric powerplants sat adjacent to Founders Park. Local developers organized the Rapid City Electric Light Company and brought in a small dynamo and about fifty electric lights in 1886. To expand service, the owners built a small dam, a diversion canal, and a hydroelectric powerplant at this location on Rapid Creek in 1888. The pond that formed behind the dam became known as "Electric Light Lake." Customers were frustrated when a variety of problems, such as inconsistent water flow, prevented the company from providing continuous power. Nevertheless, Rapid City Electric ran the plant for two decades. Dakota Power took control in 1908 and decided to build a larger hydroelectric plant at Big Bend on Rapid Creek, about twelve miles west of Rapid City, hoping to generate enough power to sell it throughout the southern Black Hills. It took four years for the Big Bend plant to become operational, but once complete, Dakota Power used the Rapid City location for auxiliary power and as a substation. As Dakota Power developed other generation facilities, it abandoned the small Rapid City plant. The city took ownership of the building in 1975 and leased it to the neighboring meat packing plant for storage space. When a fire destroyed the packing plant in 2002, the little structure sat unused and was subjected to vandalism. The plant sat just below the hill, near the bridge that crosses Rapid Creek at Founders Park; the city demolished the building in 2006.

**Meat Packing Plant:** A large meat packing plant once stood on a twenty-acre site just east of Founders Park. Local businessmen started the operation in 1909, shortly after the Milwaukee and North

Western Railroads arrived. These rail lines made Rapid City accessible to a growing number of farms and ranches, and the plant's backers wanted their business. Several Black Hills ranchers joined the cause, eager for a local outlet for their livestock instead of shipping all the way to Chicago.

Together they organized the Rapid City Packing Company and acquired land from the Crouch Line to ensure a rail connection. Starting small, the owners built a two-story structure that could handle about twenty-four beeves and twenty-five hogs per day. The plant, however, seldom operated at full capacity, requiring superintendent E. E. Hill to travel the region, encouraging farmers and ranchers to raise more livestock, especially hogs. His efforts brought slow but steady growth through the early twentieth century, and the company's Pride of the Hills products, changed later to Rushmore Brand, became well-known.

Like most businesses, the plant struggled at the start of the Great Depression. It employed only fourteen people in 1934, but then its fortunes quickly turned. The operators signed a contract to supply Civilian Conservation Corps camps. The CCC, a key part of President Franklin D. Roosevelt's New Deal, provided manual labor jobs to millions of young men between 1933 and 1942. The extra demand required the construction of a larger facility, and the robust business continued during and after World War II. As the owners enlarged the operation, they even added a truck line to distribute their products throughout the West. The good times came to an end in the 1980s. An economic downturn, limited cattle supplies, and the consolidation of larger packing houses elsewhere in the country ended the company's profitability. Black Hills Packing, as it was renamed in 1941, closed in late 1989, laying off two hundred workers and putting the plant up for sale.

A Minneapolis firm known as GFI America Inc. bought the facility and reopened it as Federal Beef Processors in early 1990. The new owner also changed the product line. From supplying a wide range of consumer goods, Federal Beef started purchasing lower-priced cows and bulls and produced hamburger for fast food restaurants and school lunch programs. The plant operated for twelve more years before a fire destroyed it in 2002. The ruins became a local eyesore as

The log pond and jack ladder of the Warren-Lamb Lumber Company, 1937. Logs floated in the pond for easier handling and were lifted into the sawmill via the jack ladder. *Black Hills National Forest Historical Collection*

the owners essentially walked away, forcing Rapid City to take them to court in 2004. Soon after, four Rapid City businessmen purchased the site and began developing upscale residences and office buildings known as Founders Park LLC.

**Warren-Lamb Sawmill:** For a time, the Warren-Lamb Lumber Company operated the Black Hills' largest commercial sawmill. Warren-Lamb's sprawling complex, which included a sawmill, a planing mill, and a storage yard, sat just east of the packing plant. The Executive Golf Course now occupies part of the company's former location. In fact, the golf course's small lake once served as the sawmill's log pond, where operators more easily handled and prepared logs for cutting by floating them in water. The logs were dumped directly into the pond from an adjacent railroad spur.

**Sawmill History:** With the construction of the North Western and Milwaukee Railroads across western South Dakota in 1907, the region began to boom. Two eastern South Dakota businessmen, W. H. Lanphere and H. W. Hinrichs, saw an opportunity to profit by selling lumber. They gained control of a tract of trees along Victoria Creek, off Rapid Canyon, imported a sawmill from the upper Midwest, and built a logging railroad into the forest. They started operating in 1908, but problems arose and the sawmill failed to make a profit. To keep the company going, Lanphere and Hinrichs brought in more investors, including C. C. Warren, a lumberman from Mississippi. Lanphere and Hinrichs soon left the firm, leaving Warren and his associates in control. Not long after, the sawmill burned. Warren brought his brother-in-law, C. T. Lamb, into the enterprise. They changed the name to the Warren-Lamb Lumber Co., rebuilt the sawmill, purchased new railroad equipment, and restarted the logging operations in 1914.

Under Warren and Lamb's direction, the company became the largest employer in Rapid City and the second largest in South Dakota. They had to deal with many challenges, however, not least of which was keeping the mill supplied with timber. This required moving the logging operations. Over the years, Warren-Lamb harvested timber in what became Custer State Park in the southern Black Hills, and along Slate and Spring Creeks in the central Black Hills. The company entered the Spring Creek drainage in 1926 and harvested most of its logs from there until about 1940.

The Depression brought even greater challenges. Demand and prices for lumber dropped dramatically, forcing the company to cut wages. With their lifestyles threatened, the workers went on strike. Hard feelings festered into violence, which included an apparent attempt to blow up the sawmill. The incident ended with the death of the supposed bomber. While the discord lasted for only about a month, the mill remained closed for over a year. All Rapid City was affected. The company returned to production as market conditions improved at the end of the 1930s. The prosperity of World War II and the years after brought big changes. High demand for lumber encouraged new sawmills to open, and the competition resulted in higher timber costs and lower lumber prices. Warren-Lamb struggled to profit. When a fire destroyed the sawmill in 1954, the company left the logging business and became a traditional lumber yard until finally closing in 1962. A few buildings remained until the 1972 flood washed them away.

**Rapid Canyon Line:** The Warren-Lamb Company worked closely with a short line railroad that went by a variety of names, but most descriptively as the Rapid Canyon Line. Attorney William T. Coad started the railroad, hoping to turn Rapid City into a mining center. When the Harney Peak Tin Company began mining tin ore around Hill City in 1886, Coad proposed that the company build a processing plant in Rapid City. His railroad would make that practical. Harney Peak Tin ignored Coad, forcing him to look for other options. It took time, but by 1891 he had decided to build his rail line up Rapid Canyon to Mystic. Not only would this route reach the mines in the central Black Hills, but it would also connect with the newly constructed Burlington Railroad at Mystic. With the railroads exchanging freight and passengers, Coad forecast reduced transportation costs for Rapid City. As he raised money and started building his little line, he found the project much more expensive and difficult to complete than he had anticipated. After thirteen years, he only managed to build a few miles of track. He went broke in 1904. His primary contractor, C. D. Crouch, purchased the line at foreclosure. Crouch managed to raise the money to finish the thirty-two-mile railroad, which included constructing over one hundred bridges. Now called the Crouch Line, it opened on 26 March 1906.

The Crouch Line seemed doomed from the start. A year after it opened, a flood washed out many of its bridges. After rebuilding, the company suffered several accidents, some of which resulted in fatalities and expensive litigation. Then the railroad failed to draw enough traffic to profit. It survived by hauling logs for Warren-Lamb and by transporting tourists, sightseers, fisher-people, and campers. As it struggled to make money, the owners threatened to close, but Rapid City businessmen, led by Warren and Lamb, saved it in 1920. World War II brought a small surge in traffic; the little railroad carried troops out of Rapid City and hauled fuel into town for the new air base. But the lack of wartime labor caused maintenance to be deferred, and the line deteriorated, leading to its abandonment in 1947.

As previously mentioned, the railroad went by many names. Rapid City residents were fond of calling it the "road of a thousand curves" and the "Dusty & Windy." Several reminders of the railroad can still be found. The Crouch Line warehouse on 7th Street is one example, but its roadbed can be found in several places along Rapid Canyon. Jackson Boulevard occupies the railroad's right-of-way on the west side of town.

## Part Two

# Downtown Rapid City, Founders Park to South Dakota School of Mines

Route Overview: From Founders Park, go to the stoplight at the intersection of Omaha and Cross Streets at the west end of the parking lot. Cross Omaha Street at the stoplight to access Main Street. Turn left (east) onto Main Street. The route will split; the eastbound lane turns into St. Joseph Street. Follow St. Joseph Street to the School of Mines for a Recommended Stop.

**Downtown Rapid City Overview:** The buildings in downtown reflect the architectural styles prevalent at each stage of Rapid City's evolution. Many of the log and wood structures that were built with the town's founding, except for the relocated Pap Madison cabin, disappeared shortly after the Fremont, Elkhorn & Missouri Valley Railroad (Elkhorn) arrived in 1886. The railroad gave a boost to the town's economy, made building materials readily available, and spurred the construction of several buildings. Many of them still stand, albeit sometimes heavily modified. Most of these structures are located in the heart of downtown, along the 600 Blocks (referring to the addresses on those blocks) of Main and St. Joseph Streets.

As the city gained more railroad and highway connections in the early twentieth century, new buildings went up a short distance from the original city core, often built in a Utilitarian style. World War II brought further growth, resulting in the construction of larger structures and the remodeling of several older, historic buildings. The Rapid City portion of this tour primarily focuses on properties included in the city's Commercial Historic District of the National Register of Historic Places.

**Preview of Rapid City's business district, Rapid, Main, and St. Joseph Streets:** Town founders envisioned Rapid Street as a key commercial location, but Main Street quickly surpassed it. A variety of early businesses opened on Main Street, with nearly every lot between 5th and 7th Streets gaining a building, even if some were mere log cabins. Two of the more impressive structures were the American House Hotel and the International Hotel that went up in 1877–1878. They occupied two of the corners at the junction of Main and 6th Streets. Deadwood merchants Harris Franklin and Ben Baer opened a very successful liquor store at another corner of 6th and Main. With the arrival of the Elkhorn Railroad in 1886, the Harney Hotel and Sweeney Hardware built impressive brick structures on the western corners of 7th and Main. They were joined by large buildings on neighboring St. Joseph Street. In particular, mining promoter Robert Flormann built the three-story Flormann Building at the southwest corner of 6th and St. Joseph and the two-story Windsor Block at the corner of 7th and St. Joseph.

**Traveling in Downtown Rapid City:** Rapid City's main thoroughfares are often quite busy, making it difficult to do drive-by sight-seeing. Because of this, the tour is organized in a block-by-block format. To take in the sights, it may be best to stop and explore on foot, particularly along the 600 Blocks of Main and St. Joseph Streets.

Mileage starts at Founders Park.

0.0 mi **Founders Park, Rapid City. Go to the stoplight at the west end of Founders Park. Cross Omaha Street at the stoplight. Go to Main Street, using Cross Street.**

0.4 mi **Intersection of Cross and Main Streets. Turn left (east).** During periods of heavy traffic, turning left from Cross Street onto Main Street can be challenging. You may wish to consider other options, such as turning right onto Main Street and then finding a convenient place to turn around toward downtown Rapid City.

0.7 mi **St. Joseph Street begins.**

0.7 mi **Halley Park:** The triangular park located between St. Joseph and Main Streets is named for James Halley, who donated much of the

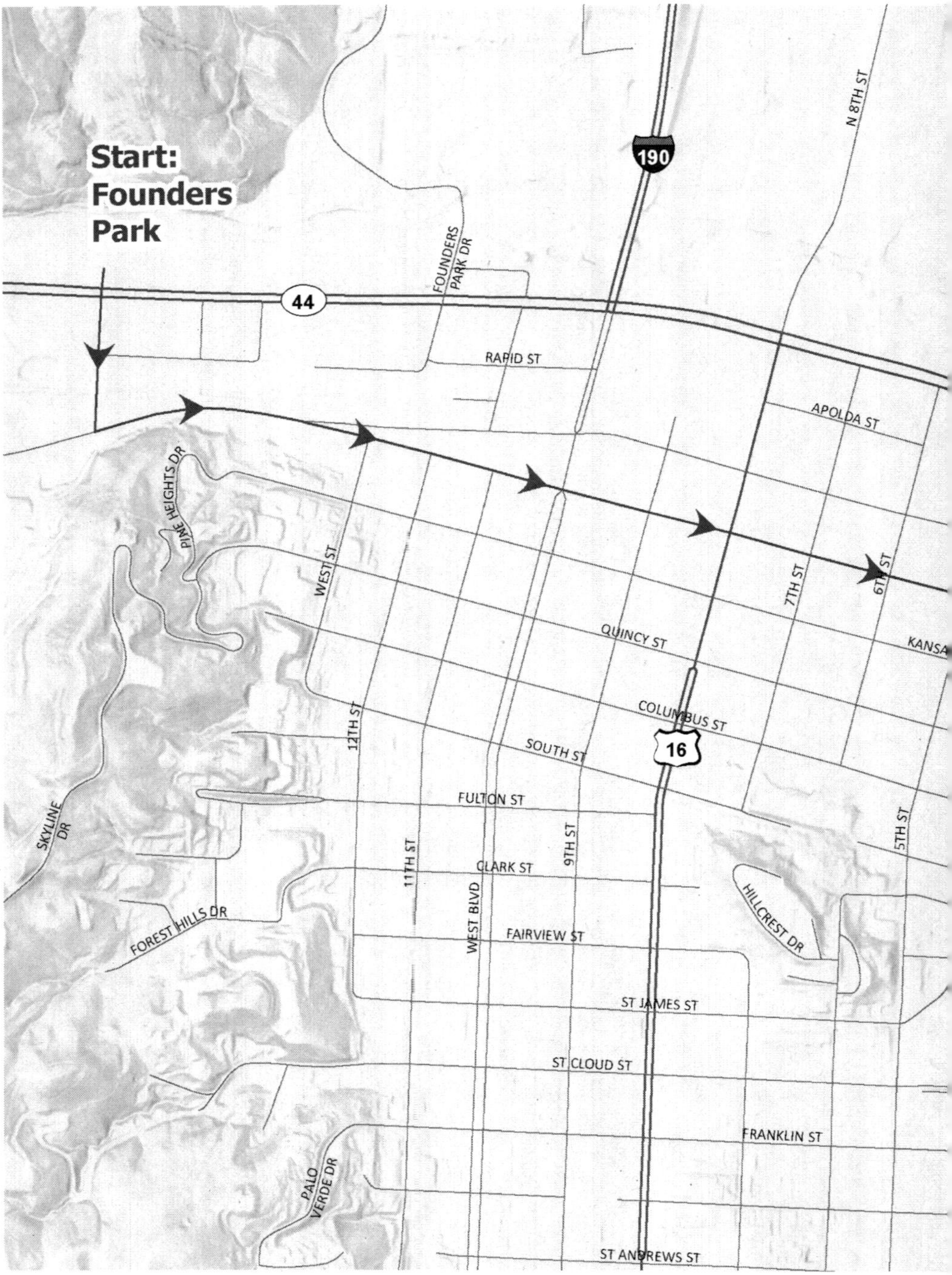
Start: Founders Park
190
N 8TH ST
FOUNDERS PARK DR
44
RAPID ST
APOLDA ST
PINE HEIGHTS DR
WEST ST
7TH ST
QUINCY ST
KANSA
COLUMBUS ST
12TH ST
16
SOUTH ST
SKYLINE DR
FULTON ST
9TH ST
5TH ST
11TH ST
CLARK ST
HILLCREST DR
FOREST HILLS DR
WEST BLVD
FAIRVIEW ST
ST JAMES ST
ST CLOUD ST
FRANKLIN ST
PALO VERDE DR
ST ANDREWS ST

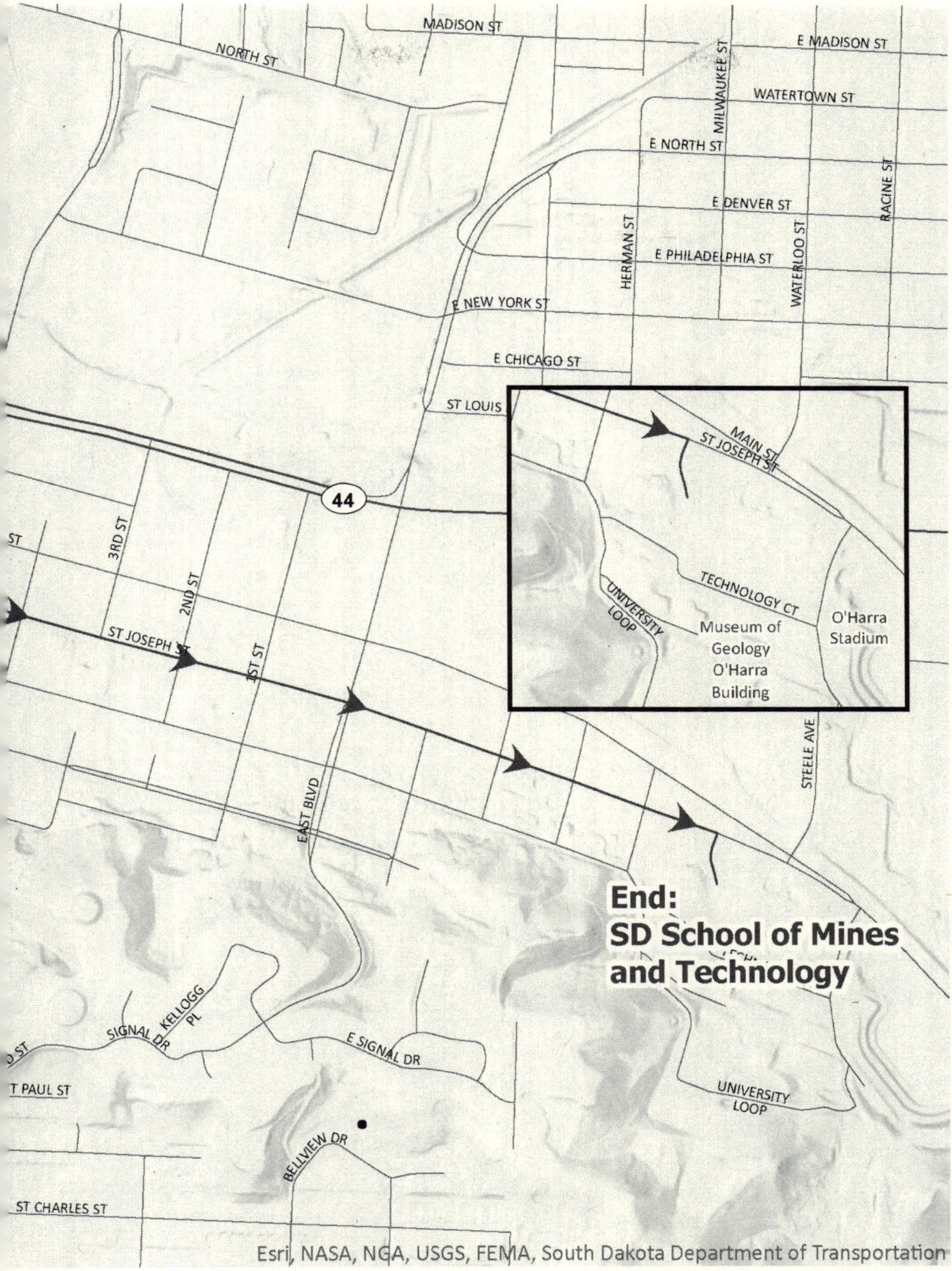
MADISON ST
NORTH ST
E MADISON ST
MILWAUKEE ST
WATERTOWN ST
E NORTH ST
RACINE ST
E DENVER ST
HERMAN ST
WATERLOO ST
E PHILADELPHIA ST
E NEW YORK ST
E CHICAGO ST
ST LOUIS
MAIN ST
ST JOSEPH ST
44
3RD ST
2ND ST
1ST ST
ST JOSEPH ST
TECHNOLOGY CT
UNIVERSITY LOOP
Museum of Geology O'Harra Building
O'Harra Stadium
STEELE AVE
EAST BLVD
End:
SD School of Mines and Technology
KELLOGG PL
SIGNAL DR
E SIGNAL DR
T PAUL ST
UNIVERSITY LOOP
BELLVIEW DR
ST CHARLES ST
Esri, NASA, NGA, USGS, FEMA, South Dakota Department of Transportation

The First Nations sculptures at Halley Park, 2022. *Author photo*

land for the park. Halley moved from Deadwood to Rapid City to open a bank in 1880 and became a prominent citizen in a variety of roles, including serving as mayor from 1884 to 1888. He died in 1920.

**First Nations Sculpture Garden:** To educate visitors about American Indian history, culture, and leadership, a sculpture garden was established in Halley Park in 2014. It currently contains the busts of four prominent Oceti Sakowin (Sioux) leaders: physician Charles Eastman, spiritual leader Nicholas Black Elk, artist Oscar Howe, and author Vine Deloria Jr.

**Rapid City Parks & Recreation Office (1938), 515 West Boulevard:** The rustic-style structure at the east end of Halley Park dates from 1938. Architect Waldo J. W. Winter designed the building, incorporating features that he had previously used in National Park Service facilities, such as the distinctive stonework and the overhanging eaves. Rapid City officials built the structure using federal money and WPA labor. A west wing was added in 1957. It originally housed the Sioux Indian Museum and Crafts Board large collection of American Indian artifacts, but the collection was moved to the Journey Museum in 1997. Rapid City Parks & Recreation uses it as an office today.

0.9 mi **West Boulevard Historic District:** An historic housing district begins at the intersection of West Boulevard and St. Joseph Street and extends south along West Boulevard. It includes forty-two blocks and hundreds of homes. A housing subdivision was first platted along West Boulevard, next to Rapid City's original townsite, in 1885. Developers knew that the Elkhorn Railroad would arrive the next year, and they correctly anticipated a need for more housing. As the area grew, the subdivision was expanded several times, giving the area a variety of architectural styles. The majority of homes date from the early to mid-twentieth century. The district was listed on the National Register of Historic Places in 1974. Many of the homeowners take great pride in their neighborhood, and the West Boulevard Neighborhood Association published *A Riding and Walking Tour of the West Boulevard Historic District*. It is available on the documents page at www.rcgov.org.

**Presidential Statues / City of Presidents:** Beginning at the intersection of St. Joseph and 9th Streets, Rapid City's downtown street corners have statues of U.S. presidents. Rapid City boosters have commissioned the works of art to honor the presidents, but also to appeal to Mount Rushmore visitors. Boosters want Rapid City to be recognized as the "City of Presidents." Each statue costs about $50,000, which is raised through private donations. The first statue went up in 1991, with regional artists receiving the commissions. St. Joseph and Main Streets have statues at six intersections, between 9th and 4th streets. Rapid City has published a guide to the statues, available at visitrapidcity.com.

**Overview of the 800 and 700 Blocks of St. Joseph Street:** These two blocks are west of the original core business district. They gained businesses and residences as the city built in that direction in the early twentieth century.

1.0 mi **Nicholas Funeral Home Building (1919), 832 St. Joseph Street:** Constructed as a funeral home in 1919, this structure was converted into an apartment building in 1926, and then into Eiler's Furs in 1959. It became an office building in the early twenty-first century, and currently houses Rensch Law. The building's height, symmetrical façade, dormers, pitched roof, and multi-paned windows reflect its Colonial Revival design. This style, meant to resurrect architecture from the American colonial period, is most frequently associated with buildings from 1910 to 1930.

**Hill Apartments (1920), 814 St. Joseph Street:** This building provided more residential infrastructure west of downtown Rapid City. When completed in 1920, it contained apartments and a chiropractic office. It features a Craftsman style with overhanging eaves, exposed rafters, and double-hanging windows. Sears, Roebuck and Company catalogs often featured similar designs in the early twentieth century.

**Rapid City Business College (1920), 804–806 St. Joseph Street:** As American businesses grew in the early twentieth century, so did the demand for people with office skills. To meet this need, private "business colleges" opened across the country, offering a practical education in bookkeeping, shorthand, typing, and penmanship. In 1910, Mr. & Mrs. G. W. Brown, who had operated schools elsewhere, opened the Rapid City Business College on the second floor of the Sweeney Building on Main Street. Despite regularly enrolling about thirty students, the Browns sold the school in 1913. H. W. Hawley eventually acquired it and erected this three-story, institutional-type structure with simple Art Deco features in 1920. The college only used the second floor. Rapid City Steam Laundry occupied the first floor, and the third floor was reserved for meeting rooms. Despite competition from three other private business colleges in South Dakota, Hawley did well in the 1920s as people from throughout the Black Hills took his classes. The financial problems of the Depression, however, cut enrollment, and the school closed. The structure soon sold, becoming known as the Lewis Building. A mission-style storefront was later added.

1.1 mi **Federal Building (1914), 731 St. Joseph Street:** The post office was a vital part of any frontier town. Not only did it keep residents connected to home, but it also served as a community center. Rapid City's first post office was described as a "nondescript structure" presided over by town founder John Brennan. As the city grew, the post office moved from location to location. Residents wanted a structure that reflected their city's importance in the early twentieth century, especially since Deadwood received a large post office and federal courthouse in 1907. With South Dakota representative Eben W. Martin taking the lead, Congress finally authorized a federal building for Rapid City in 1913. When it opened in May 1914, the structure's Classical Revival (or Neoclassical) design gave it a look common to federal buildings and made Rapid City residents swell with pride. One newspaper stated that Rapid City's post office was larger than those of similarly sized cities. After the federal government moved out in the mid-1970s, the building became an office complex.

1.2 mi **Security Building (1928), 704 St. Joseph Street:** When the Security Savings Bank opened in 1908, it was located on 7th Street, but it then moved into this Utilitarian structure with Art Deco ornamentation in 1928. The word "Security" can be seen over the central entrance. H. W. Hinrichs helped open the bank as Rapid City got an economic boost with the arrival of the North Western and Milwaukee Railroads in 1907. Hinrichs had previously lived in eastern South Dakota and expected big things of Rapid City. Besides opening the bank, he worked with W. H. Lanphere to establish a sawmill and logging business that eventually became the Warren-Lamb Lumber Co.

1.2 mi **Overview of the 600 Block:** Several buildings went up along the 600 Blocks of St. Joseph and Main Streets with the arrival of the Elkhorn Railroad in 1886. One observer called it the "great building boom of 1885–1888." A number of these structures survive, although some are heavily modified.

**Driving/walking instructions for the 600 Block:** The heavy traffic through the 600 Blocks of St. Joseph and Main Streets makes it difficult to follow the tour narrative from your vehicle. Stopping and taking a brief walking tour may be the best way to appreciate the many historic structures. For ease of understanding, the buildings on the left (north) side of the street will be discussed first, followed by those on the right (south) side.

### North side of the 600 Block of St. Joseph Street:

**Buell Building/Lakota Block (1888–1889), 630 St. Joseph Street:** Known as the Buell Building today, the structure on the northeast corner of St. Joseph and 7th was originally called the Lakota Block. Investors in the new Lakota Bank, which included Black Hills pioneer Valentine McGillycuddy, built the block in 1888–1889. The bank occupied the corner office. Wentworth Rice, a local contractor and part-time architect who was best known for building mine and mill structures, designed the building. He apparently had no set architectural style in mind but created arched windows and doorways with bricks and sandstone to give it a Romanesque flair. The corner onion dome tower and other decorative elements give it a Queen Anne style. McGillycuddy, as president of the bank, personally installed the distinctive stained glass in the 7th Street windows. On completion, a Rapid City paper described it as the "handsomest block in the city." Additions in 1901, 1915, and 1925 extended the building along 7th Street.

Besides the Lakota Bank, the structure's first occupants included J. W. Collins's photography studio, the Sprando restaurant, and John L. Spayde's mercantile. A variety of offices occupied the second floor, including attorneys, real estate agents, and dentists. Turnover among the building's tenants was high. The Lakota Bank closed at the onset of the Panic of 1893. The structure's most famous occupants included the U.S. Weather Service and the attorney Charles Buell, who rented a second-floor office in 1891 and purchased the block in 1901, giving the building his name.

**"The Italianate Trio" (1886), 618–608 St. Joseph Street:** More commercial buildings went up east of the Lakota Block during the 1880s boom. A series of one-story structures was built next to the Lakota Block in 1888, but the two-story buildings a little farther

St. Joseph Street in Rapid City, undated. The Buell block is visible on the right; Sweeney Hardware on the left. *South Dakota State Historical Society*

down St. Joseph Street stand out for their historic integrity. Known as the "Italianate Trio," the three buildings were built in 1886. Their Italianate characteristics include decorative cornices and tall, narrow windows. A variety of businesses have occupied these buildings over the years, but small grocery stores stand out as some of the earliest occupants.

**Hotel Alex Johnson (1928), 6th & St. Joseph (523 6th Street):** Rapid City's most prominent landmark sits next to the Italianate Trio. To help promote Rapid City's tourism and commercial interests, Chicago and North Western Railroad (C&NW) vice president Alex Johnson commissioned the construction of this namesake hotel in 1927, the same year the work on Mount Rushmore began in earnest. The hotel's architectural details are meant to highlight the area's scenery and culture. The decorative timbers at the top of the eleven-story structure are often seen in buildings with a Tudor de-

The Hotel Alex Johnson, ca. 1971. *Watson Parker Ghost Town Notebooks, Leland D. Case Library for Western Historical Studies, Black Hills State University*

sign; in this instance, they represent the nearby mountains. The terra-cotta Indian-head medallions above the second story windows reflect the region's Native traditions. When dedicated in 1928, the hotel was billed as the largest in South Dakota and the "showplace of the West." It has hosted a variety of dignitaries, including presidents and actors, and was featured in Alfred Hitchcock's classic 1959 film, *North by Northwest*.

The hotel's main floor once housed transportation companies that offered tours of the Black Hills, including Paul Bellamy's Black Hills Transportation Company. A Rapid City businessman and tourism enthusiast, Bellamy purchased five eighteen-person buses with convertible tops and started offering tours that lasted from one to four days in 1926. For over twenty years, his red buses with bison insignias on the doors were common sights around the Black Hills. By the time he sold in 1949, most vacationers used their own autos, hurting his patronage.

**South side of the 600 Block of St. Joseph Street:**

**Windsor Block (1886), 629 St. Joseph Street:** Across the street from the Buell Building is the Windsor Block. Robert Flormann, a Black Hills pioneer and business promoter, built this corner Italianate-style building in 1886. It has been heavily modified over the years, and for a time the second floor was covered with white siding and a piano keyboard sign promoting Plummer's Piano and Organ. A recent owner has restored the building. Today it houses Presidential Pawn.

The Windsor Block is one of at least three buildings Flormann constructed in downtown Rapid City in the mid-1880s. But he was also connected with several mining ventures that turned out to be investment schemes. Somehow Flormann always managed to profit while investors did not. Regardless of his mixed legacy, his positive contributions to Rapid City are noteworthy.

**Hall Building (1886), 623 St. Joseph Street:** Next to the Windsor Block is another Italianate structure built in 1886. Besides its tall, narrow windows, it has a couple of unique features. One is the decorative cast-iron front on the first floor that reportedly came from the Union Foundry and Pullman Car Wheel Works of Pullman, Illinois. The Pullman Company primarily manufactured Pullman Palace Cars for the nation's railroads, but the foundry also cast iron products for general use. The building's other unique feature is a stone panel centered between the upstairs windows that features a lion's head. Its significance is unknown. A Rapid City newspaper once commented on its "decorative quality," but failed to explain it.

**Flormann Building (1884), 601 St. Joseph Street:** A one-story building sits on the corner lot across from the Hotel Alex Johnson. Robert Flormann originally built a three-story building there in 1884. It was the largest and tallest building in Rapid City for forty-four years, until the construction of the hotel in 1928. Always a risk-taker, Flormann built the imposing structure prior to the arrival of the Elkhorn Railroad, anticipating the upcoming boom. It was one of at least three buildings that Flormann built in downtown Rapid City. Its stone construction and sheer size caused it to stand out among the much smaller, mostly wooden buildings around it. Structural problems, however, forced the removal of the top two floors in 1958. The historic first story is hidden behind the modern façade.

**Intersection of 6th and St. Joseph, Rapid City City Hall (1903–1904), 616 6th Street:** One half-block south of St. Joseph Street is a one-story brick building that served as city hall for over thirty-five years. It included council chambers, a police department, a fire department, and a city jail. A tall bell tower once stood behind it. When it opened in early 1904, the *Rapid City Journal* praised its practicality, including the possibility that a larger structure could be built around it, and for less than $1,800. That, however, never happened. The city hall moved out, and the building has remained basically unaltered.

**Intersection of 6th and St. Joseph, Rapid City High School:** Three blocks south of the intersection of 6th and St. Joseph is the location of what was known as Rapid City's "new" high school, constructed in 1913. The building gained notoriety when President Calvin Coolidge used it as his "Summer White House" while vacationing in the Black Hills in 1927. From it he issued his famous announcement, "I do not choose to run for President in nineteen twenty-eight." Many believed Coolidge could easily win a second term and were shocked by the declaration. The building was later renamed Coolidge High School. It was damaged by a 1970 fire that started in neighboring Washington Elementary School (no one was injured) and both schools were subsequently demolished.

**Duhamel Building (1908), 530 6th Street, across 6th Street from the Hotel Alex Johnson:** Peter Duhamel started a successful ranch on the open range east of Rapid City in 1879 and prospered until homesteaders claimed the land. He and his son, Alex, then opened a hardware and housewares business in downtown Rapid City, known as the Duhamel Company, in 1905. With the business's success, they built a large department store in the Chicago Style from 1907 to 1909. By using a load-bearing steel frame, Chicago Style buildings featured extensive commercial spaces and large windows. When the Duhamel Building opened, a *Rapid City Journal* reporter raved about its size and beauty, but wondered how the windows would be cleaned.

Alex managed the business and continually expanded its activities. When he opened a custom saddle shop, Duhamel saddles became world famous. To enhance Rapid City's western image and bolster the tourist trade, Alex established the Cowboy and Indian Trading Post, selling locally made Indian blankets, moccasins, and other handcrafts. To further promote American Indian traditions, Duhamel asked Lakota holy man Nicholas Black Elk to create an educational program featuring Native dances and ceremonies. The result was the Duhamel Sioux Indian Pageant, presented nightly in front of the store during the summers, beginning in 1927. Lakota men and women were the main performers, but a promotional piece described it as having "Sioux, Crow and Cheyenne Indian war dances." The show's popularity encouraged Duhamel to move it to other venues. When Duhamel acquired ownership and began offering tours at Sitting Bull Crystal Caverns on the road to Mount Rushmore in 1934, he staged performances both at the cave and in Rapid City. He eventually moved the shows entirely to the cave. The performances initially drew enthusiastic crowds, but interest in the Indian Pageant waned over the years. The Duhamels ended the show in 1957. The renamed Duhamel Western Store in downtown Rapid City closed in 1985.

1.3 mi **Overview of 500 and 400 Blocks of St. Joseph Street:** The buildings on the 500 and 400 Blocks of St. Joseph Street sit just outside of the main business district and were built after Rapid City's early twentieth-century boom had ended. The earliest standing structure dates from 1929, and the architectural styles are mostly Utilitarian, designed for function over beauty. An example of Utilitarian style is the small two-story structure at 510 St. Joseph Street, just down the block from the Duhamel Building. It was constructed in 1930.

**South Dakota Stockgrowers Association, 426 St. Joseph Street:** This Utilitarian building is noteworthy for the neon sign on its rooftop. Installed in 1958, the twenty-foot-high mounted cowboy has become a Rapid City landmark. More significantly, it reflects the importance of the ranching industry to the community. Stockgrowers began meeting in Rapid City in 1880, and from the late nineteenth into the early twentieth centuries, an annual stockmen's celebration was the city's biggest event. It included parades, horse races, and shooting contests. Hard times in the 1920s and 1930s ended this early event, but post-World War II prosperity persuaded the chamber of commerce's agricultural council to sponsor a livestock show called the Black Hills Winter Show in 1959. A rodeo was added in 1978, and the Black Hills Stock Show and Rodeo has become one of the city's largest events.

**Motor Service Co. (1929), 402 St. Joseph Street:** As automobiles became more common, garages and auto agencies went up just outside the downtown business district. These areas generally had lower property values and taxes, allowing businesses to buy substantial amounts of land. The Motor Service garage is one example. Built in 1929, it has a Utilitarian style with Art Deco influences.

1.5 mi **Courthouse Square (1922), 300 St. Joseph Street:** The Pennington County Courthouse complex dominates the 300 Block of St. Joseph Street. The structure on the Block's west end, dating from 1922, is the third courthouse to occupy that location. The first went up in 1882 and burned in 1897. The second courthouse was built soon after but was demolished in 1922. This structure replaced it. The building's symmetry and paired columns reflect its Beaux Arts architectural style, commonly used in public buildings in the early twentieth century to reflect status and importance.

1.8 mi **East Boulevard:** This street marks the eastern end of Rapid City's original 1876 townsite survey.

2.4 mi **South Dakota School of Mines and Technology, 501 East St. Joseph Street. Enter the campus at a convenient location for a Recommended Stop.** There are three possible places to park on the School of Mines campus. The Surbeck Entrance provides access to a large parking lot just off St. Joseph Street. When school is out of session, it is a good place to start a tour of campus, including a visit to the Museum of Geology. When school is in session, the parking lot is generally crowded. Visitor parking is available along the lot's south side, but the spaces are often occupied. The Gold Entrance, about 0.2 miles east of the Surbeck Entrance off St. Joseph Street, is another option, especially for easier access to the Museum of Geology. The Gold Entrance turns onto University Loop. Follow the signs to the Museum of Geology inside the O'Harra Building. Visitor parking is available along the side of the building. The third possible place to stop is by O'Harra Stadium. Access to its parking lot is approximately 0.3 miles east of the Surbeck Entrance. This location is where the chlorination plant and smelter once stood, which are discussed below.

The Dakota Territory legislature established the School of Mines in 1885 to teach mining on a scientific basis. Despite some initial struggles, the school has become a national leader in science, engineering, technology, and math education. Today it offers twenty undergraduate and twenty-eight graduate degree programs, with an enrollment of nearly 2,200 undergraduate students and over 300 graduate students.

**The School of Mines' Early Years:** Soon after John Brennan and his associates established Rapid City in early 1876, they realized that much of the region's mining activity took place in the northern Black Hills, a good distance from their nascent community. Not to be thwarted, they joined with other Rapid City boosters to look for ways to develop a local mining industry. One of their efforts was to begin promoting a school of mines. Not only would the professors train a new generation of mining men, but they could also identify and analyze new mineral locations, especially in the central and southern Black Hills, where the boosters believed there must be undiscovered mineral deposits. The resulting development would cause Rapid City to boom, turning it into the regional service and mercantile center the founders visualized.

To make the school a reality, Rapid City resident and representative to the territorial legislature John W. Nowlin submitted a bill during the 1883 session to establish a mining school and allocate $10,000 to support it. The local newspaper rallied to the cause, extolling the school's benefits and comparing its potential to the success of Colorado's School of Mines in Golden. The Deadwood newspaper saw the situation differently. Disliking any potential threat to that town's importance, the editor went after the logic behind the school, stating that mining men learned the trade by working in a mine, not in a classroom. Despite Deadwood's protests, the territorial legislature passed the bill, only for it to be vetoed by the territorial governor, Nehemiah Ordway, who saw it as a waste of money. Two years later, a new governor, Gilbert Pierce, signed a similar bill into law. When the boosters laid the cornerstone of the school's first building in August 1885, they saw it as an important step in Rapid City's development.

The school got off to a rough start, however. The newly appointed trustees wanted instruction to begin in the fall of 1886; it was instead delayed until 1887, partly due to an inability to hire faculty. As Ruth Anne Stymiest commented in her *Centennial* history of the school, "Men were not anxious to leave a secure position to take charge of a school that had no registered students, lacked funds, and was located in a place remote from creature comforts." Nevertheless, Franklin R. Carpenter agreed to become the school's first dean in late December 1886. Having previously taught and worked as a mining engineer in Colorado, Carpenter had moved to the Black Hills to investigate tin deposits. As he finished his work, Rapid City businessmen hired him to survey the region's mineral resources. That project gave Carpenter a good knowledge of the area and persuaded the trustees to offer him the job.

Carpenter managed to hire more faculty and welcomed twenty students to the school's first class. Encouraged, the trustees persuaded the territorial legislature to construct a second building and purchase more equipment. Even so, faculty resigned—including Carpenter in 1889—few students enrolled, and funding proved scarce. The trustees soon discovered that Deadwood's newspaper editor had been right: most mining men learned about mining on the job, and few wanted a college degree. In fact, the school failed to graduate a single student through most of the 1890s. Faculty helped keep the doors open by testing ore samples and investigating new ways to treat gold ores. The situation gradually changed as the idea of an academic mining education gained traction. The school again graduated students in 1901, and the programs grew in the years that followed. After an uncertain beginning, the school eventually thrived because of supportive trustees, such as Valentine McGillycuddy, the work of capable instructors, including C. C. O'Harra, and the arrival of more students.

**School of Mines Museum of Geology:** The geology museum dates from the school's founding. In the summer of 1885, just as construction on the first building got underway, Gilbert Bailey, a mining man with the Harney Peak Tin Company, donated his collection of more than 5,000 fossil and mineral specimens to the school. Over the years, the school's collection has grown to reflect the geological diversity of the Badlands, the Black Hills, and western South Dakota. The museum is housed on the third floor of the O'Harra Building, near the center of campus. It is well worth a visit.

**O'Harra Stadium, Site of Chlorination Plant and Smelter:** The school's football field and O'Harra Stadium are located a quarter mile east of the main part of campus, off of St. Joseph Street. In the late nineteenth and early twentieth centuries, this area was home to a chlorination plant, a cyanide mill, and a smelter, each geared toward separating gold from ore albeit using different processes. In addition to promoting the School of Mines, local leaders also recruited mining men to build two of the processing plants; an ambitious School of Mines student built the third. All three were built east of town for the nearby rail connections and the availability of water from Rapid Creek.

**Welcome Chlorination Plant:** The Black Hills Mining and Chlorinating Company built the first processing facility in the area of the football field in 1892. A year prior, the Rapid City Board of Trade had learned that the Black Hills Mining Company's investors had leased the Welcome mining claims in the Ruby Basin District, west of Lead. Inspired by the success of the Golden Reward Company's chlorination plant in Deadwood, the men behind the Black Hills Mining and Chlorinating Company wanted to erect their own plant. Rather than place it in Deadwood or near their mines, however, the company's backers announced that they would accept proposals from any town interested in hosting the plant. In essence, they believed that several Black Hills communities might want the financial benefits of a gold mill and would be willing to bid for it. The Rapid City Board of Trade responded with a winning bid that included $10,000 in cash, land for the plant, and free water. Richard Lake and James Halley, directors of the First National Bank in Rapid City, also advanced a $10,000 line of credit.

Construction of the Welcome Chlorination Plant began in November 1891. The *Rapid City Journal* quickly proclaimed that a "new era" was at hand and that the chlorination plant would "encourage the erection of smelters" that could treat ores from the central Black Hills. The Welcome plant began operating in early 1892. Early optimism throughout Rapid City soon turned to despair as reports emerged of the company failing to make a profit. Some blamed the machinery for not running smoothly, but the bigger issue was the cost of transporting ore from Lead to Rapid City. The plant closed in 1893, one year after opening. The First National Bank gained control of it at a sheriff's sale.

The bank hoped to sell to a new owner, but the economic depression in 1893 made money scarce, discouraging potential buyers. When prosperity finally returned in 1897–1898, a new investor appeared. Colonel H. Day, owner of the Gilt Edge Mine in Galena, bought the plant and brought in John E. Rothwell, known as the "father of the chlorination process," to fix it. After nine months of work and an estimated $12,000 expended, the steam whistle again blew in July 1898, bringing a hearty cheer from the gathered crowd. The plant closed again just ten months later, in May 1899. The company's expenses overwhelmed what little wealth could be extracted from the Gilt Edge's low-grade ore. The chlorination plant reverted to the First National Bank and would never operate again.

**Clevenger's Cyanide Plant:** After the chlorination plant's failure, most people in Rapid City saw little value in the abandoned works, but School of Mines student Howell Clevenger sensed opportunity. By 1900, mining engineers had shown that the recently developed cyanide method for gold recovery was superior to other processes. It had not been successfully tried in the Black Hills, however. Clevenger decided to build an experimental plant next to the chlorination works in the summer of 1900. He had previously tested the old plant's tailings and discovered that they carried gold that the chlorination process had missed. In between classes, Clevenger built a series of small tanks and filled them with tailings and cyanide. He ran his little plant for about a year, treating around 8,000 tons of the tailings and producing over nine pounds of gold, worth more than $3,000. His achievement impressed many in town, especially since the sand tailings had previously been used for building purposes. One observer estimated that over $2,000 of gold had gone into constructing the courthouse. Oddly, Clevenger's success did not inspire Rapid City investors to build a cyanide plant—with a smelter operating successfully in Deadwood, boosters saw it as the preferred method for precious metal recovery, and they got their opportunity to bring a smelter to town just as Clevenger wrapped up his operation.

**National Smelter:** Mining promoter Dr. H. H. Muggley of Galena organized the National Mining & Smelting Company and announced plans to build a smelter to treat ore from his Bullion Mine in 1901. Town leaders, led by Mayor Chauncey Wood and businessman Tom Sweeney, offered Muggley a $4,000 cash bonus, twenty-five acres of land next to the chlorination plant worth $9,000, the abandoned plant valued at $50,000, and what was described as a "$25,000 mansion" in an "exclusive residential district." The generous offer caught the attention of people throughout the Black Hills. The Deadwood paper commented that the "people of Rapid City are after a smelter and are liable to succeed."

At a June 1901 groundbreaking ceremony, Mayor Wood forecast that the smelter "would be the opening wedge" in Rapid City's economic "resurrection." Under the direction of Theodore Knutzen, a smelter man with many years' experience, the new plant contained several innovations, including steel construction for strength and fire resistance. After expending an estimated $250,000, Knutzen put the plant's furnaces "in blast" in April 1902. As smoke began rising from the large smokestack constructed on the hill just behind the smelter, Rapid City residents scurried to the plant to gather small pieces of waste known as slag. In July 1902, after only four months of operation and just as success seemed at hand, Muggley left and the National Smelter closed. The most likely explanation is that the Bullion Mine produced too little valuable ore.

It seemed the Horseshoe Mining Company would come to the rescue when it bought the smelter soon after. The company had consolidated several claims west of Lead in the early 1890s and had produced some gold before closing in 1901. D. E. Murphy of Milwaukee

The National Smelter at the South Dakota School of Mines, ca. 1901.
*William J. Collins Collection, Leland D. Case Library for Western Historical Studies, Black Hills State University*

and E. M. Holbrook of Chicago then purchased the company and ambitiously expanded operations. They began building a large cyanide plant at the mine site, remodeled a gold mill in Pluma, and purchased the National Smelter. In another fit of enthusiasm, the *Rapid City Journal* called the smelter's sale the "greatest thing" the town had ever known.

The Horseshoe Company, however, ran the smelter intermittently, then shut it down in early 1903, blaming the cost of shipping the ore. Chicanery on the part of the owners was the real problem. Murphy and Holbrook had little interest in actually producing gold; they instead bilked stockholders, purchasing the smelter to give the company an appearance of greatness, hoping to persuade more people to invest. As soon as Murphy and Holbrook had enriched themselves, they left the Black Hills, leaving a financial mess for others to figure out. New managers eventually reorganized the property as the Mogul

Mining Company, but they saw little value in the smelter and kept it closed.

After the large plant sat idle for two years, C. D. Crouch, the owner of the Rapid Canyon Line railroad, leased it in 1905. He believed that a successful smelter would encourage miners to develop the untapped mineral resources in the central Black Hills, which would in turn create traffic for his soon-to-be-completed railroad. Crouch renamed the plant the Standard Smelting Company and reportedly spent $60,000 to remodel it. Despite the modifications, the smelter again failed to operate successfully and closed after about six months. When South Dakota state historian Doane Robinson visited the plant in late 1907, he recognized that the smelter had never worked properly and estimated that each ton of slag contained about two dollars in gold, meaning the 100,000 tons of accumulated slag may have contained as much as $200,000 of gold.

**Creation of O'Harra Stadium:** Despite both the chlorination works and the smelter failing, the superstructures remained, standing next to each other just below what was known as Smelter Hill and slightly above where O'Harra Stadium is today. The chlorination plant disappeared in 1910, when a Denver company scavenged the machinery. The Mogul Company, however, kept the smelter on standby for nearly ten years, during which time School of Mines students occasionally operated it to gain practical experience. Once it became evident that the smelter would never return to full-time service, the Mogul Company sold it in 1912 to a Rapid City firm that wanted the structural steel. The building remained standing until it was sold again in 1919. The new owner dismantled it, including taking down the tall smokestack that had become a Rapid City landmark. After the smokestack's concrete base was removed in the mid-1960s, only a sandstone foundation remained.

With both plants gone, the surrounding area became what locals described as a wasteland. People dumped garbage there, a pond formed in a low-lying area, and a neighboring farmer let his pigs roam through the debris. That began to change when Dr. O'Harra purchased the land to create an athletic field for the school in 1930. Over the next few years, students and volunteers slowly cleared the land.

The federal government gave the project a boost when it became one of Pennington County's first relief projects in 1932. The WPA eventually stepped in and finished the field and stadium in 1938, contributing approximately $70,000 of the $132,000 total cost. To take advantage of the hill on the stadium's south side, the former site of the chlorination plant and smelter, the workers carved terraces where people could park their cars to watch sporting events.

**"Tower on the Hill":** In 1983, British artist Andrew Leicester built a five-story wood-framed tower over the smokestack's foundation. Known as "Tower on the Hill," it included several panels discussing Black Hills history. Because of deterioration and safety concerns, the tower was dismantled in 2008, but for a quarter century it stood as a Rapid City landmark. A wind turbine currently sits on top of Smelter Hill.

## Part Three

# Downtown Rapid City, School of Mines to Dinosaur Park

Route overview: The tour reverses course and travels west on Main Street. When leaving the School of Mines, turn left (west) and follow Main Street through Rapid City to its intersection with Mt. Rushmore Road. Turn left (south) onto Mt. Rushmore Road/US 16. Travel on Mt. Rushmore Road five blocks to the junction with South Street. Turn right onto South Street and follow it to West Street. Turn right onto West Street and follow it to Quincy Street. Turn left onto Quincy Street. It becomes Skyline Drive as the road ascends Hangman's Hill. Follow Skyline Drive to Dinosaur Park for a Recommended Stop.

Mileage starts from Surbeck Entrance to the School of Mines.

0.0 mi **Surbeck Entrance, Rapid City.**

1.0 mi **Railroad yards:** The Fremont, Elkhorn & Missouri Valley Railroad (Elkhorn) established the rail yards north of Main Street in 1886. The Chicago and North Western Railroad (C&NW) eventually absorbed the Elkhorn and continued to use these yards until selling its Black Hills operations to the Dakota, Minnesota and Eastern Railroad (DME) in 1986. The DME then sold to the Rapid City, Pierre & Eastern in 2014. The railroad primarily hauls bentonite out of Colony, Wyoming. The C&NW built the five-stall roundhouse.

**Overview of 200, 300, and 400 Blocks of Main Street:** These three Blocks sit outside of Rapid City's main commercial district, on less valuable land. This made it attractive to light industries and automobile businesses. Four buildings still exist that reflect this mixed use, all of which were built in the 1920s.

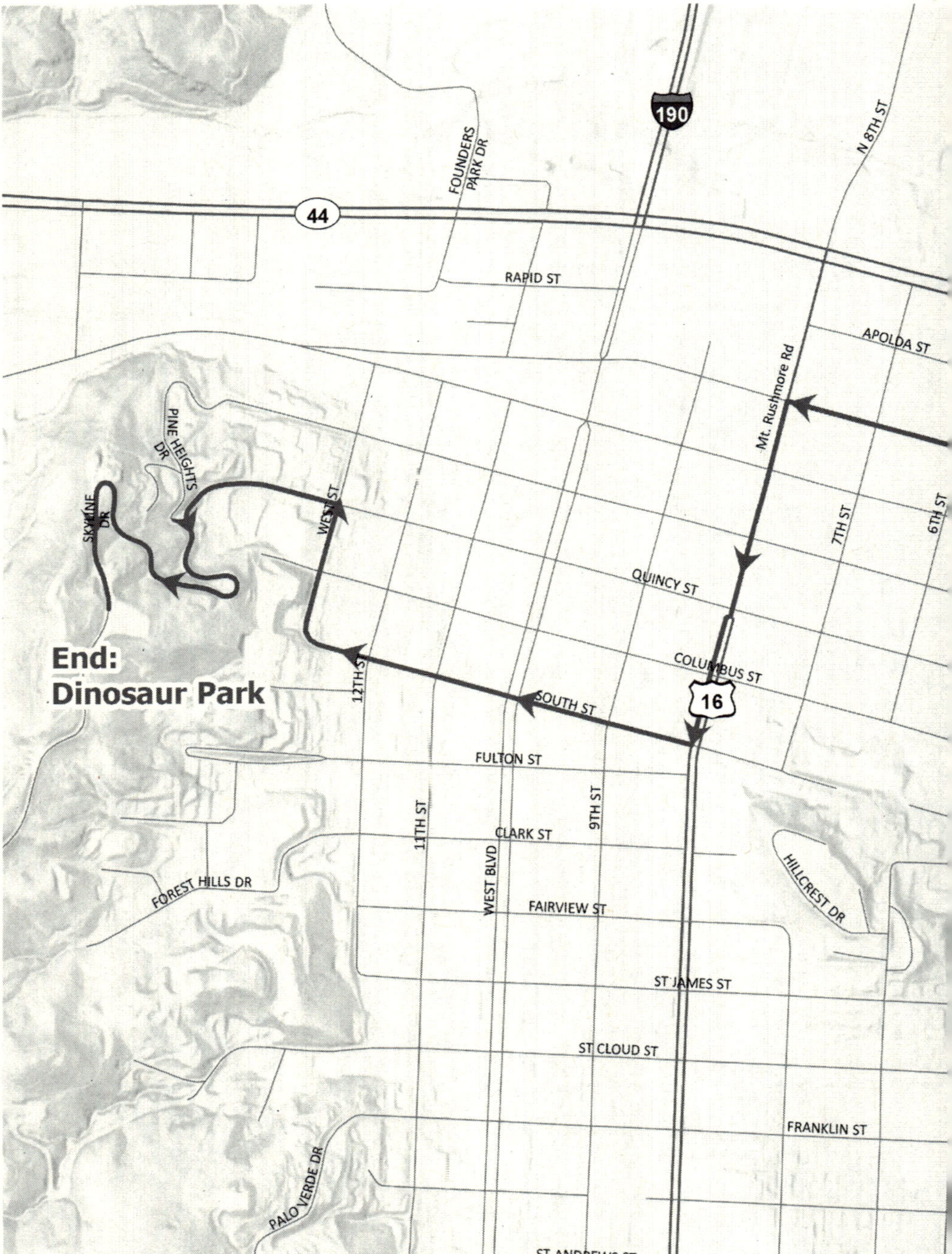
190
N 8TH ST
FOUNDERS PARK DR
44
RAPID ST
APOLDA ST
Mt. Rushmore Rd
PINE HEIGHTS DR
SKYLINE DR
WEST ST
7TH ST
6TH ST
QUINCY ST
COLUMBUS ST
End:
Dinosaur Park
12TH ST
16
SOUTH ST
FULTON ST
11TH ST
9TH ST
CLARK ST
WEST BLVD
FOREST HILLS DR
HILLCREST DR
FAIRVIEW ST
ST JAMES ST
ST CLOUD ST
FRANKLIN ST
PALO VERDE DR
ST ANDREWS ST

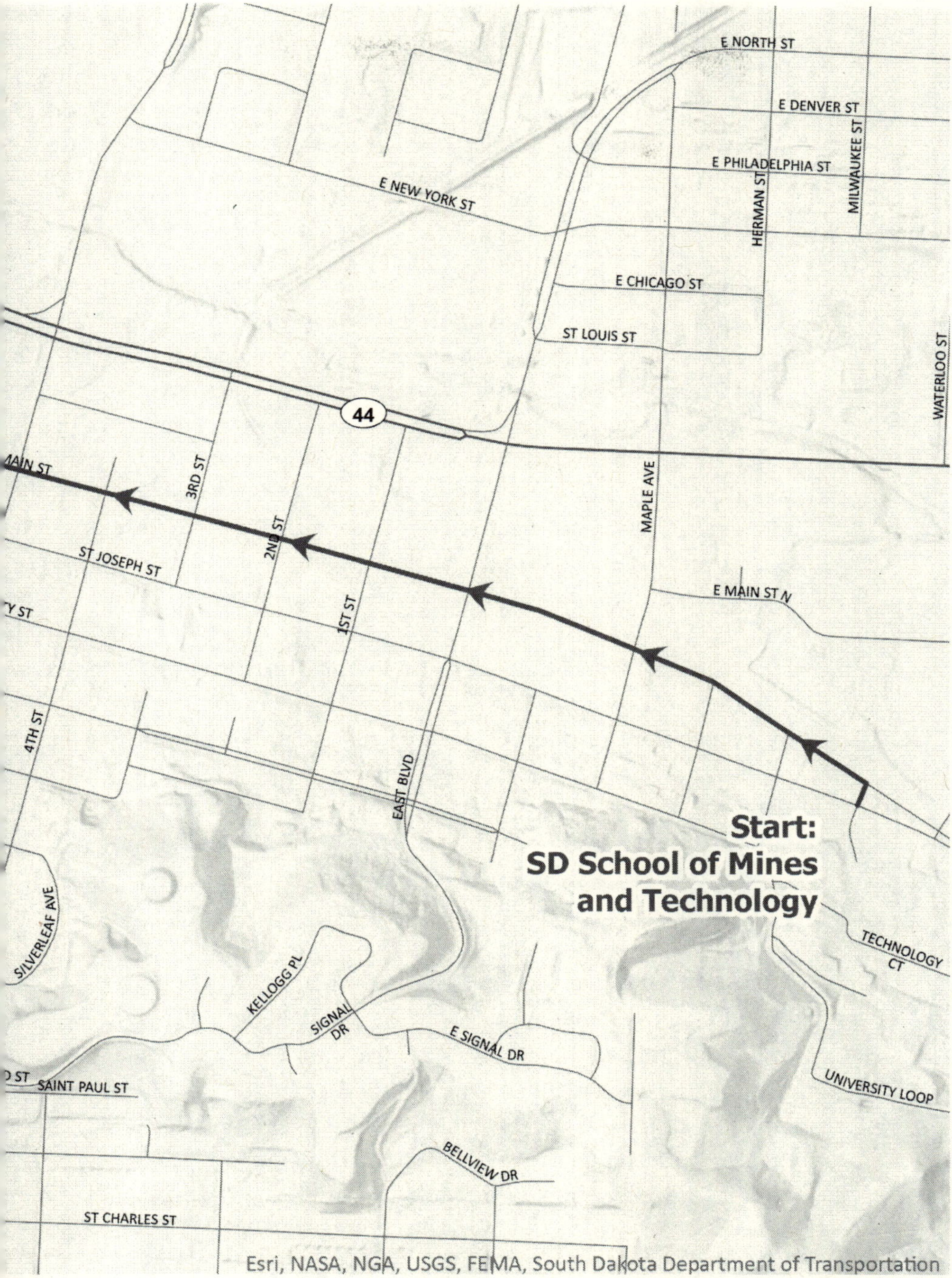
E NORTH ST
E DENVER ST
E PHILADELPHIA ST
MILWAUKEE ST
HERMAN ST
E NEW YORK ST
E CHICAGO ST
ST LOUIS ST
WATERLOO ST
44
MAIN ST
3RD ST
2ND ST
MAPLE AVE
ST JOSEPH ST
E MAIN ST N
1ST ST
4TH ST
EAST BLVD
Start:
SD School of Mines
and Technology
SILVERLEAF AVE
TECHNOLOGY CT
KELLOGG PL
SIGNAL DR
E SIGNAL DR
UNIVERSITY LOOP
SAINT PAUL ST
BELLVIEW DR
ST CHARLES ST
Esri, NASA, NGA, USGS, FEMA, South Dakota Department of Transportation

1.6 mi **Fairmont Creamery (1929), 201 Main Street:** Fairmont Creamery started operations in Rapid City in 1926, three years before constructing this Industrial-style building. The exterior bricks were made in Belle Fourche. The pink sandstone was mined at the Evans Quarry near Hot Springs. The interior contains glazed blocks and a sloped floor to allow for efficient cleaning. Fairmont Creamery sold a variety of dairy products, including ice cream, butter, and milk. To promote its business, the company installed a twenty-five-foot-high milk bottle on the roof. The Rapid City store was part of a national chain established in Fairmont, Nebraska, in 1884. As the company expanded, it moved its headquarters to Omaha in 1907. A large Fairmont Creamery building still stands in Omaha's Warehouse District.

A national food conglomerate bought Fairmont Creamery in the latter half of the twentieth century and closed many of its outlets, including the Rapid City plant, in 1971. The empty building fell into disrepair. The Rapid City Historic Preservation Commission listed it as an endangered historic property in 2002. Since then, it has been redeveloped and now hosts a variety of small businesses.

1.7 mi **Servall Uniform building (1929), 312 Main Street:** This Art Deco structure was built for Rapid City Laundry in 1929 and has been expanded over the years. The center door and the two windows on each side are from the original building.

**Dean Motor Service building (1929), 329 Main Street:** This Commercial-style structure from 1929 was one of several auto dealerships and garages constructed in this part of Rapid City.

1.8 mi **"Parts Central" or Casper Supply Co. (1946), 415 Main Street:** Casper Supply Company started in Casper, Wyoming, in 1917, selling tools and auto parts. It slowly expanded to ten stores, with the Rapid City branch opening in 1930. After weathering the Depression, the business flourished during and after World War II. To handle the increased trade, the company built this structure in 1946, one of several buildings that went up during the postwar boom. The rounded windows and decorative brickwork give it an Art Deco look. It became a Parts Central store in 1968.

1.9 mi **5th & Main Furniture (1947), 430 Main Street:** This large Utilitarian-style building was built for a Gambles Hardware store in 1947. To make room for the new building, the two-story International Hotel had to be demolished. The hotel had originally been located at the corner of 6th and Main in 1878 and was moved to this corner to make way for the Elks Building in 1911. When it opened, the International was described as one of the very best hotels in the Black Hills, but it deteriorated over the years. It primarily served as a long-term rooming house at this location. Its demolition and the construction of the Gambles store came during the postwar boom. As the Gambles store went up, the *Rapid City Journal* claimed that it marked an "epoch in the growth of Rapid City."

1.9 mi **1876 Blockhouse Location, Intersection of 5th & Rapid:** Rapid City residents built a two-story blockhouse near the intersection of 5th and Rapid, one block north of this location, in 1876. Hostilities with American Indians had peaked in the months after the Battle of the Little Bighorn, and the trails and settlements on the edges of the Black Hills were among the Lakotas' favorite targets. When four people died near Rapid City in August 1876, many of the town's two hundred residents fled. Eighteen men and one woman stayed and built a small log fortress or blockhouse for protection. No further deaths were reported near Rapid City. The blockhouse stood until the logs were appropriated for a jail in 1879.

1.9 mi **Overview of the 500 Block of Main Street:** This Block sat near the center of Rapid City's earliest business district, but once the town boomed in the second half of the 1880s the city's growth centered more on the 600 Block of Main Street. It was not until the first half of the twentieth century that significant development returned to the 500 Block.

**First Chance, Last Chance Saloon (1906–1908), 508 Main Street:** This Italianate commercial structure was built to house the First Chance, Last Chance Saloon sometime between 1906 and 1908. It is the oldest existing building on the 500 Block of Main Street. Located on the edge of downtown, it offered the first chance to have a

Rapid City's Main Street, 1907. The building on the far right is the Clower Block, originally known as the Evans-Poznansky-Morris Block. *William J. Collins Collection, Leland D. Case Library for Western Historical Studies, Black Hills State University*

drink when arriving and the last chance to have one on the way out, according to its owner. The slogan must have been persuasive; the saloon was known for drawing rowdy crowds. The structure underwent several modifications over the years, but a recent owner has restored it to its original appearance.

**Shops at Main Street Square (1947), 512 Main Street:** This two-story Utilitarian structure was built as a Sears store in 1947, the same year as the Gambles Hardware store, during Rapid City's postwar boom. Today it houses the "Shops at Main Street Square."

**Yankton House (1877–1901), 515–523 Main Street:** In this area in June 1877, Daniel J. Stafford and Grove Corwin, described as enterprising and experienced hotel men, built a two-story hotel out of hand-hewn logs and named it the Yankton House, after their hometown. It was one of the town's largest structures, and Pennington County officials opened their offices there when Rapid City became county seat later that year. Stafford only operated the hotel for about eight months before selling it to H. L. Holcomb. The Yankton House went through several remodels and ownership and name changes, becoming variously known as the Holcomb House, the Sherman House, and the Merchants Exchange Hotel. When it was demolished in 1901, the *Rapid City Journal* lamented its loss, explaining that the hotel had witnessed everything from births to deaths.

2.0 mi **Elks Theater (1911–1912), southeast corner of 6th & Main, 512 6th Street:** Located at a central downtown location, this corner has attracted businesses since Rapid City's earliest days. After selling out of the Yankton House in early 1878, Daniel Stafford purchased a building located here and remodeled it into a two-story hotel he named the Stafford House. Two years later, he sold it to P. B. McCarthy and a partner. McCarthy soon took sole ownership and expanded the business, changing its name to the International Hotel, which occupied this location for the next thirty-two years. McCarthy promoted the International as a "First-Class" facility, with the Northwestern Express, Stage and Transportation Company using the hotel as its headquarters. Stages to Deadwood and other Black Hills locations left from its front door from 1882 until 1888. As the years passed, larger and fancier hotels went up in Rapid City, such as the Harney Hotel in 1886. By the time the Elks Lodge began looking for property in 1910, the International had lost much of its prestige, and McCarthy turned the location over to the Elks, with the understanding that his building could be moved two blocks east on Main Street.

When construction of the Elks Building began in August 1911, several hundred Elks arrived from across the state to lay the cornerstone. By using sandstone from Hot Springs and locally made bricks, the architect created tan walls that simulate stucco and adobe, giving it a Spanish Colonial Revival look. Opened in 1912, the Elks Building provided an important entertainment center for the burgeoning community. It contained a theater and small shops on the first floor, offices on the second, and Elks Lodge rooms on the third. Its construction coincided with the period of growth following the arrival of the Milwaukee and North Western Railroads in 1907–1908.

2.0 mi **Overview of the 600 Block of Main Street:** Since the town's founding, the 600 Block of Main Street has attracted a variety of businesses to become Rapid City's most vibrant commercial district. Historic bank buildings anchor two of the corners, highlighting the Block's stature. It also has buildings that span several eras of construction, from 1885 to 1930. For clarity, the structures on the right (north) side of the street are discussed first.

**The right (north) side of Main Street's 600 Block:**

**Statue at corner of 6th & Main:** The eight-foot-tall statue in front of the Prairie Edge is titled "Hunkayapi" or "Tying on the Eagle Plume." It depicts a Lakota woman elder placing the first eagle plume in the hair of a young girl as she prepares for the Lakota naming ceremony. Created by Sturgis artist Dale Lamphere, the work highlights the importance of women in Lakota culture.

Lamphere's piece replaced a statue that Glenna Goodacre, a noted artist from Santa Fe, New Mexico, had created for the Prairie Edge when it opened in 1993. Titled "He Is They Are," it depicted a warrior with his hands bound behind his back, with the inscription, "The Sioux and the Plains Indians were moved from their homelands and placed on reservations. Though their 'hands are tied,' the dream of their homeland remains." Many Native people found the work insulting and degrading. The owners of the Prairie Edge responded to these concerns and hired Lamphere to create a replacement work that better portrays the wisdom, dignity, and pride of Native people. Goodacre's piece is now displayed at the Nedra Matteucci Galleries in Santa Fe.

**Prairie Edge & Sioux Trading Post (1886), 606–608 Main Street:** Fred Evans, Felix Poznansky, and Louis Morris built the two-story brick Italianate building at the corner of 6th and Main as the Elkhorn Railroad arrived in 1886. Originally known as the Evans-Poznansky-Morris Block, it replaced three wooden structures that the men had owned at the same location. The new building housed the L. Morris & Co. dry goods store, also known as the California Store; Poznansky's Montana Store, which sold clothing and dry goods; and Franklin, Baer, and Haller's liquor store. Franklin and Baer had operated a similar business in Deadwood and wanted to capitalize on Rapid City's prosperity.

The building's occupants changed frequently. Franklin and Baer moved out when South Dakota adopted prohibition in 1890. Poznansky closed his store the following year. These departures allowed L. Morris & Co. to expand before it eventually moved across the street. To fill the void, one of the structure's more famous occupants moved in. Once alcohol again became legal, "Big Jack" Clower opened a saloon in the corner location, and the building became known as the Clower Block in 1900. The drinking establishment soon gained a notorious reputation as a place where cowhands frequently "cut loose." A. J. Behren moved his furniture business next to Clower's saloon in 1905, and a series of businesses would follow, such as appliance and piano stores. Neglect finally caused the building to fall into disrepair, but Ray Hillenbrand came to the rescue. He restored the structure to its former grandeur and opened the Prairie Edge & Sioux Trading Post, an outlet for American Indian products, in the early 1980s.

**Rapid City Fire Department (1915), 610 Main Street:** Next to the Prairie Edge is the Rapid City Fire Department building. Built in 1915, it is an example of the Chicago style of architecture popular at the time. It has a steel framework, a symmetrical appearance, and three-part windows on the second floor. Despite a substantial amount of brick construction, wood buildings still dominated downtown Rapid City in the early twentieth century, so placing the fire hall in the center of town made sense.

**Firehouse Wine Cellar and Mercantile (mid-1920s), 616, 618, and 620 Main Street:** Next to the fire hall are three similar-looking structures that date from the mid-1920s. While architecturally described as Utilitarian, they have other stylistic influences. For instance, the building at 620 Main Street has windows divided into three parts, resembling the Chicago style. Restaurants, grocery stores, clothing stores, and auto parts dealerships operated out of these locations over the years. One notable enterprise was Henry Behren's mortuary. He used a wooden structure at 618 Main Street from 1879 to 1925 and occupied the new building from 1925 to 1939. The Firehouse Brewing Company, having opened in the old fire department building in 1991, eventually acquired the structures for its auxiliary businesses.

**The left (south) side of Main Street's 600 Block:**
**Sculpture at the southwest corner of 6th & Main:** Titled "Mitakuye Oyasin (We Are All Related)," this bronze sculpture grew out of a competition the Rapid City Public Arts Committee held for American Indian artists in 1994. Richard Under Baggage won the competition with a two-dimensional drawing that Dale Lamphere then turned into this sculpture. According to Lamphere, the work "symbolizes the interrelation of all creation." An anonymous donor provided the funding. When it was dedicated in 1996, eight-inch bronze castings were sold to raise money for the Black Hills Pow Wow Association.

**Neugebauer's Fine Jewelry (1915), 601 Main Street:** The Classical Revival-style building at the corner of 6th and Main is the third building to occupy this site. Rapid City founder John Brennan built the first structure, the American House Hotel, in early 1878. His experience working at Denver's American House prior to relocating to the Black Hills had convinced him of a hotel's value, both for the owner and the community. Within two months of laying out Rapid City, he opened a hotel in a small log structure on Rapid Street, which he later replaced with a two-story frame hotel at this location that he promoted as the "largest and best appointed in the Black Hills." He also advertised that it had the largest stable in the city. To further advance his business, Brennan became agent for the Sidney & Black Hills Stage, Mail & Express Company, making his hotel the company's headquarters from 1878 to 1886. With the Sidney stage stopping at the American House and the Northwestern stage stopping at the International Hotel, across the street, the intersection of 6th and

Main Streets served as Rapid City's transportation center until the Fremont, Elkhorn & Missouri Valley Railroad came to town in 1886. The railroad's arrival convinced Brennan that Rapid City needed a hotel that better reflected its new importance. He leased out the American House and helped finance the Harney Hotel farther down Main Street. When fire destroyed the American House in February 1888, it housed five businesses on the main floor, including two saloons, while apartments occupied the second floor.

Even though Brennan moved his hotel to the 700 Block of Main Street, the 600 Block retained its stature as Rapid City's most important commercial district. The owners of the Pennington County Bank recognized the value of this location and built an ornate brick and sandstone structure in 1888. Rapid City already had two banks, and the opening of a third reflected the town's growing prosperity in the wake of the Elkhorn Railroad's arrival. In January 1915, a fire spread from a neighboring store into the bank, causing the walls to crack and collapse. The bank's owners quickly rebuilt this Classical Revival-style structure, with columns, rectangular windows, and a symmetrical design.

The Depression forced the Pennington County Bank to close in 1932. As the economy improved, the bank reorganized and reopened as the Rapid City National Bank. It eventually outgrew this space and relocated to a larger structure in 1942. The building has housed a succession of businesses until Neugebauer's Fine Jewelry opened in 1995.

**Dakota Power Building (1915) and Haines Building (1915), 603, 605, and 607 Main Street:** A two-story Italianate structure was built at 603 Main Street in the 1880s. For a time, it housed the New York Store, specializing in ladies' clothing. Dr. E. Farlow, a local physician, eventually acquired it, and it became known as the Farlow Building. In 1907, John C. Haines demolished two frame structures next door to build a two-story stone-and-brick building for his "Bee Hive" clothing store. That same year, he became president of the Dakota Power Company. In 1915, a fire destroyed both the Bee Hive and the Farlow Building. Haines built these Utilitarian-style commercial structures on the ashes, reopening the Bee Hive as the Haines Store and using what had been the Farlow Building as the Dakota Power Company's office and showroom.

The two buildings hosted a variety of businesses after Haines left. J. C. Penney moved into the Dakota Power Building in 1927 and operated there for the next half century, eventually expanding into the neighboring structures and placing green paneling across the front. When J. C. Penney moved to the Rushmore Mall in 1978, the buildings sat empty until Stan Adelstein restored them in 1996.

**Dreamland Theater (1887), 609 Main Street:** This Romanesque building with a heavy brick façade and arched windows was constructed in 1887, during Rapid City's first boom. It has housed numerous businesses over the years. In the early twentieth century, it was home to Coolidge & Brothers, a Chicago chain store that sold hardware and farm supplies. From 1908 to 1918, it served as the Dreamland Theater, where upwards of five hundred people could watch silent movie stars like Mary Pickford and Charlie Chaplin. After the theater closed, clothing, drug, and jewelry stores called the building home before J. C. Penney expanded into the space.

**Flynn's Book Store (1891), 611 Main Street:** This Romanesque building was constructed in 1891. The L. Morris Company, which called itself the "House of Bargains," moved in not long after and stayed until the summer of 1923. Flynn's Book Store then opened and developed a substantial business over the next forty-five years, promoting itself as "The Book Store of Rapid City." Hardware and interior design stores followed.

**Behrens Furniture (1891), 613 Main Street:** When it was built in 1891, the structure at 613 Main Street probably had a Romanesque design. The vertical and geometric Art Deco design elements were most likely added in the 1930s. As with many downtown buildings, several businesses have come and gone, including Behrens Furniture, grocery stores, and a shoe store.

**McNamara Bros. Building (1914), 615 Main Street:** John and Edward McNamara built this Utilitarian-style commercial building with Neoclassical elements in 1914. The brothers arrived in Rapid City sometime around 1885 and opened a newsstand in the lobby of the post office. As their business grew, they moved into a frame building that stood on this lot in 1893. They replaced that structure with this two-story brick building, renting out the upstairs for professional offices. They developed the largest bookstore and stationery shop in western South Dakota before selling to H. L. Bongers and T. J. Flynn (of Flynn's Book Store) in 1917. Besides running the bookstore, the two brothers had several other business and real estate interests, including a stake in the Rapid River Milling Company.

**J. J. Newberry Building and Rise Building (1926–1937), 617–619 Main Street:** When Carl Rise first arrived in Rapid City in 1910, he opened an optometry office in the Harney Hotel but soon ventured into commercial photography and photo finishing. Needing more space for his growing business, he built this three-story Utilitarian building in 1926. Rise ran his photography business out of the basement and main floor and rented out the second and third floors. With a knack for innovation, Rise soon developed one of the largest mail order photo finishing businesses in the Midwest. He also became well known for taking photos of Black Hills scenery and for placing promotional signs along area highways. Besides running Rise Studio, he served on the city council.

As work on the Rise Building began, an early piece of Rapid City history came to light. Two structures occupied the lot, and as workers removed the siding, they discovered that one of them was a log cabin. The *Rapid City Journal* promptly claimed that it was the oldest remaining log building in Rapid City. A later *Journal* column even claimed that Calamity Jane had once lived there. Research, however, seems to indicate that Charles Roberts erected the log structure as a restaurant and bakery in 1877, and since the Pap Madison cabin at the Journey Museum is believed to be from 1876, Roberts's cabin was probably not the oldest.

Rise constructed the building next door, at 617 Main Street, for the

J. J. Newberry Company, a five-and-dime chain, and sold both buildings to that enterprise in 1937. To match the Chicago-style structure that had been previously built just to the west, he incorporated many of the same elements, such as large first-floor windows and three-part second-floor windows. The new building replaced a single-story wooden structure dating from Rapid City's early years that had housed meat markets run by Charles Schuster and Earl Bowden. J. J. Newberry stayed at this location until 1962, and then a Ben Franklin variety store opened in the two storefronts. When Rise sold the buildings, he transferred his photo business to Mike Beckers, who ran a pharmacy next door. Beckers turned Rise Studio into Rushmore Photo and came to specialize in producing picture postcards.

**Beckers Drug (1890s), 621 Main Street:** The modern façade on this building covers the brick front of a Utilitarian structure that probably dates from the late 1890s. For nearly eighty years, it housed a drug store that passed from one owner to another. Michael Beckers held it the longest. Known as Doherty Drug when Beckers started working there in 1934, he took control in 1937 and renamed it Beckers Drug. He ran it for thirty-six years, until his death in 1973.

**Republican Block (1886), 623–627 Main Street:** Named for a newspaper published on the second floor, the Republican Block was constructed in 1886. The first floor held a variety of businesses, including Billy Blair's saloon and M. Willsie's real estate agency. A Woolworth's five-and-dime store opened at 627 Main Street in 1923 and expanded into the neighboring buildings. The Woolworth's became the Republican Block's longest occupant, staying for nearly sixty years.

**Woolworth's (1885), 629 Main Street:** Built in 1885, this structure has been extensively remodeled and is described today as having a Postmodern design. It housed Fallon Drug and other businesses before Woolworth's moved in. After Woolworth's closed, a "99 cent" store opened. Along with the Republican Block, local businessman Stan Adelstein took control of the building and remodeled it in 1995.

**First National Bank of Rapid City (1915), 631 Main Street:** Like the bank at 601 Main Street, this building features a Classical Revival style, with columns, rectangular windows, and a symmetrical design. Bank owners R. C. Lake and James Halley were praised for building the first brick structure in Rapid City at this location in 1882. Ironically, it was torn down when structural problems threatened its integrity. The current structure replaced it in 1915.

2.1 mi **Overview of the 700 Block of Main Street:** This block sat on the edge of Rapid City's core business district. While it did not attract as many businesses as the 600 Blocks of Main and St. Joseph Streets, two prominent enterprises once occupied the corners of 7th and Main. No historic structures survive.

**Sweeney Hardware, 701–707 Main Street:** Sweeney Hardware sat on the southwest corner of 7th and Main. At 45,000 square feet, it covered five city lots. Tom Sweeney built the three-story Italianate-design building for his hardware business just as the Elkhorn Rail-

Thomas Sweeney's hardware store on the corner of 7th and Main, undated. *William J. Collins Collection, Leland D. Case Library for Western Historical Studies, Black Hills State University*

The Harney Hotel, undated. *Black Hills National Forest Historical Collection*

road arrived in 1886. According to one story, Sweeney, a consummate "go-getter," arrived in town flat broke and borrowed fifty cents from freighter Fred Evans, which gave him the start to create a highly successful hardware business. Part of his success came from promotion. He was famous for putting up highway signs that said, "Tom Sweeney wants to See You." Besides running his store, Sweeney worked diligently to help Rapid City prosper. He assisted with several projects, including the Rapid Canyon Line railroad, and he often spearheaded community celebrations. One observer called him the most popular man in town. His building stood until a 1997 fire destroyed it. Modern construction now occupies the site.

**The Harney Hotel:** A three-story Italianate-style hotel sat across Main Street from Sweeney Hardware. Hoping to capitalize on the surge of travelers that came with the Elkhorn Railroad's arrival, town founder John Brennan and other investors spent over $40,000 to build the Harney Hotel in 1886. It quickly became known as the finest hotel in the region, an honor it held until the Hotel Alex Johnson went up in 1927–1928. The Harney was remodeled over the years and demolished in 1973.

**Water fountain:** A water fountain sits at the Harney Hotel corner. The National Humane Alliance of New York City gave the fountain to Rapid City to provide water for horses and dogs. When installed at the intersection of 7th and Main in 1911, the fountain had a light on the top. It was moved to Halley Park when the city paved Main Street in 1921. In recent years the fountain was restored and replaced near its original location.

**Who's Hobby House Sign, 715 Main Street:** The neon sign promoting Who's Hobby House has been a Rapid City landmark since 1951. It has also been listed on the National Register of Historic Signs. The "Who" name is an acronym of the original owner's name, William Howard Ostenberg.

2.2 mi **At the intersection of Main Street and Mt. Rushmore Road, turn left (south) onto Mt. Rushmore Road/US 16. Travel five blocks to the junction with South Street.**
South Street was the southern boundary of Rapid City's original 1876 survey.

2.5 mi **The McGillycuddy House (1887), 727 South Street:** Black Hills pioneer Valentine McGillycuddy built this Victorian-style home in 1887. Prior to moving to Rapid City in 1886, he had accompanied the 1875 Newton–Jenney Expedition (sent to map the Black Hills and determine their material value) and supposedly became the first white man to scale Black Elk Peak, then known as Harney Peak. He had also worked at the Pine Ridge Agency as a physician and Indian agent. While in Rapid City, he served as mayor, president of the School of Mines, and president of the Lakota Bank. He left town in 1902 and traveled extensively before dying in California in 1939 at the age of ninety. His ashes were interred near the top of Black Elk

Peak. McGillycuddy's house was altered extensively after he left, and it eventually fell into disrepair. Historic Rapid City began restoring it in 2011.

2.5 mi **Turn right onto South Street. Follow it to West Street.**

2.8 mi **West Boulevard:** South Street crosses West Boulevard and the upper end of the West Boulevard Historic District.

3.0 mi **Turn right onto West Street and follow it to Quincy Street.**

3.1 mi **Intersection of West Street and Quincy Street. Turn left onto Quincy Street. It becomes Skyline Drive as the road ascends Hangman's Hill. Follow Skyline Drive to Dinosaur Park. Recommended Stop at Dinosaur Park.** If these directions are confusing, the goal is to reach Skyline Drive and Dinosaur Park, regardless of the route.

**Skyline Drive:** Rapid City promoters had long envisioned this mountaintop, known as Hangman's Hill, as the ideal place for a road and a park. They felt that the views of the city and the mountains would draw visitors. The Rapid City Chamber of Commerce and the city persuaded the WPA to build the access road, and about 150 men started it in December 1933, although the workforce fluctuated often. It took just over two years to complete the project, with the last guardrails going up in early 1936.

6.0 mi **Hangman's Hill:** Skyline Drive passes a dead tree known as the "hanging tree" or "Hangman's Tree." On 20 June 1877, amid an epidemic of horse thefts in Rapid City, a sheriff's posse came across three men, Red Louis Curry, Doc A. J. Allen, and Kid James Hall, camped along a road north of town with a half dozen horses. The posse suspected them as horse thieves, confirmed when four of the animals were identified as property of the stage company. The three men were promptly arrested and put under guard in a log cabin, but not for long. Masked vigilantes appeared around midnight and escorted the prisoners to this ridge. They picked a hilltop location to make sure that

The Hanging Tree, 2022. *Author photo*

all could see and understand the price horse thieves pay. As events unfolded, Curry and Allen confessed but claimed Hall was innocent. Nevertheless, the vigilantes hanged all three. The men were buried in a single grave and a board was placed on top that said, in part: "We're bound to stop this business or hang you to a man; For we've hemp and hands enough in town to swing the whole damn clan." Some sources state that the original Hangman's Tree wasted away, but to keep the story alive, city promoters replaced it. The current tree is on private property. In recent years the hill has become better known as Dinosaur Hill.

6.2 mi **Recommended Stop at Dinosaur Park:** Local businessmen, including Rapid City pioneer George Mansfield, donated the land for the road and a city park. Before long, the park grew beyond the usual picnic tables and hiking trails to become what Mansfield later described as "one of the most unique, attractive and educational recreation spots anywhere." Apparently inspired by an exhibit at the 1933–1934 Chicago World's Fair, the secretary of the Rapid City Chamber of Commerce presented the idea of developing a dinosaur park. To make the proposal more appealing, the chamber framed it as a memorial to Dr. C. C. O'Harra, who had served as president of the School of Mines for nearly twenty-five years before passing away in early 1935. Beyond his reputation as an expert geologist, he had become well known and universally admired as a Rapid City supporter and a Black Hills history enthusiast.

With the WPA providing funding, technical advice, and labor, the city appointed local sculptor Emmet Sullivan to construct five dinosaurs. By covering a framework of steel tubing and wire mesh with concrete—a technique he had devised—Sullivan made good progress until he became angry with WPA officials and walked off the job, taking the Tyrannosaurus rex's teeth with him. He claimed that he had made the teeth on his own time. Once the dispute was settled, he placed the teeth where they belonged. Several possible dates exist for the project's completion. The WPA's dedication plaque states 1936, but the city dedicated the park on 1 June 1937, and it was not finished until 1938. After the construction was completed, Sullivan and his wife ran the gift shop, selling several items he made. The city took control in 1967, and Dinosaur Park was added to the National Register of Historic Places in 1990.

**Communication towers and the Alice Gossage Monument:** Dinosaur Hill ridge has become a convenient location for radio and television towers, many of which went up in the 1950s. One of those towers sits where the Alice Gossage Monument was once located. The Rapid City Fortnightly Club successfully spearheaded a drive to place a concrete pillar, a sundial, a bronze plaque, and several benches just off Skyline Drive in 1938. After two decades, the monument became ignored and neglected. A television station then took control of the property. While the plaque and sundial were relocated to Halley Park, the concrete column was pushed over and laid next to a tower for years. In the summer of 2024, a group of citizens interested in preservation, along with the Rapid City Parks and Recreation Department, the Black Hills Historical Society, and the Journey Museum, rescued the tower and moved it to the Journey Museum. It now sits next to the Pap Madison cabin on the museum grounds. More information about Alice Gossage and the monument is available in the Journey Museum write-up.

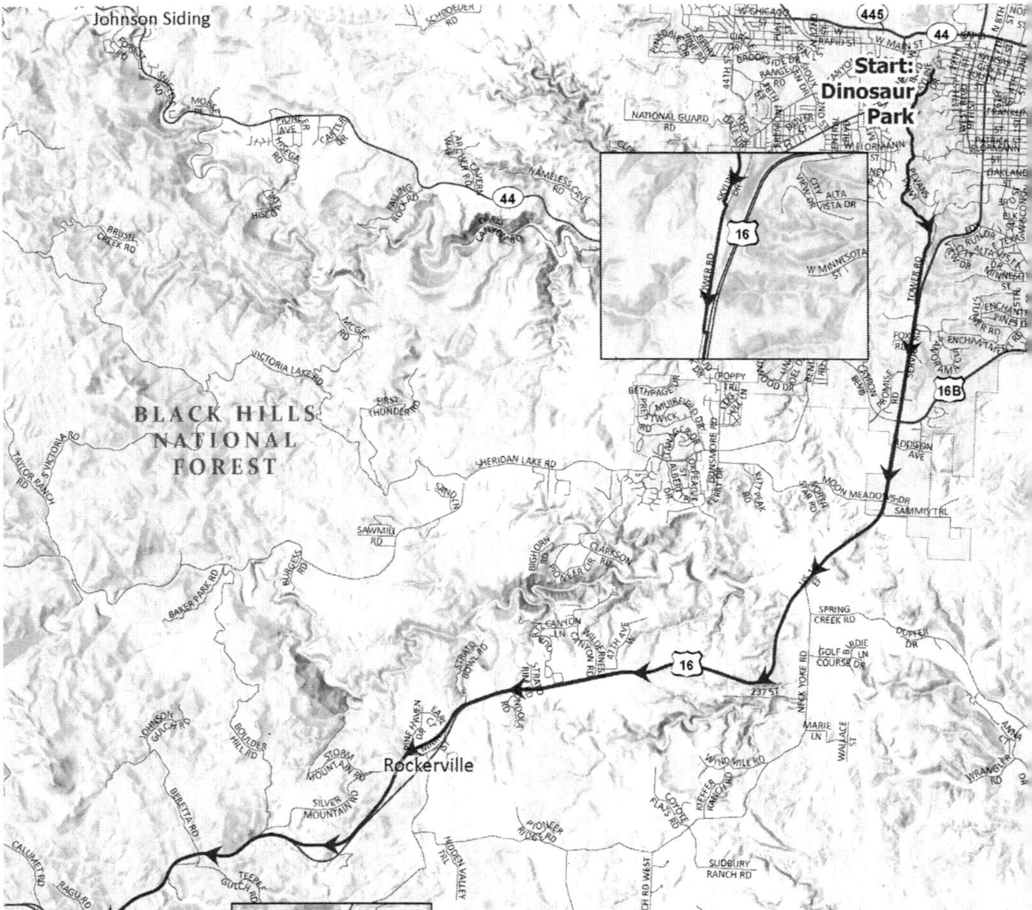
Johnson Siding
Start: Dinosaur Park
BLACK HILLS NATIONAL FOREST
Rockerville
Old Keystone
Keystone and Holy Terror Mines
SWANZEY ST
THIRD ST
Keystone
End: Keystone
16
16A
16B
40
44
244
445
SHERIDAN LAKE RD
VICTORIA LAKE RD
NATIONAL GUARD RD
TOWER RD
MOON MEADOWS DR
SPRING CREEK RD
NECK YOKE RD
SILVER MOUNTAIN RD
STORM MOUNTAIN RD
PINE HAVEN DR
BOULDER HILL RD
JOHNSON GULCH RD
BEBETTA RD
TEEPEE GULCH RD
CALUMET RD
RAGU RD
COSMOS RD
OLD HILL CITY RD
HIDDEN VALLEY TRL
HART RANCH RD WEST
SUDBURY RANCH RD
PINE GROVE RD
MURPHY RD
140 AVE
Esri, NASA, NGA, USGS, FEMA, South Dakota Department of Transportation

## Part Four **Keystone**

Route Overview: Travel south on Skyline Drive. Merge onto US 16 Service Road and then onto US 16. Take US 16 south to its intersection with US 16A. Follow US 16A to Keystone. At the stoplight, intersection of US 16A and Reed Street, turn left into old Keystone for a Recommended Stop in front of the Keystone–Holy Terror Mine, next to the "Rock Shed."

Mileage starts at Dinosaur Park.

0.0 mi **Dinosaur Park, Rapid City.**

0.5 mi **Petrified Forest Trailhead:** This trailhead marks the former location of a log-shaped building that served as the concession stand for a tourist attraction known as the Skyline Petrified Forest, or Fossil Forest. Rapid City residents had long known that petrified wood could be found on this hillside, and some people took pieces home. As Skyline Drive neared completion in the late 1930s, city boosters, led by George Mansfield, believed that opening a second attraction on the road would create a premier tourist destination. Mansfield arranged for the chamber of commerce to take control of the land, and for nearly twenty-five years the chamber hired a variety of staff to operate the attraction. Earl Brockelsby, the founder of Reptile Gardens, probably controlled it the longest, but other concessionaires included Ed Boylan, owner of

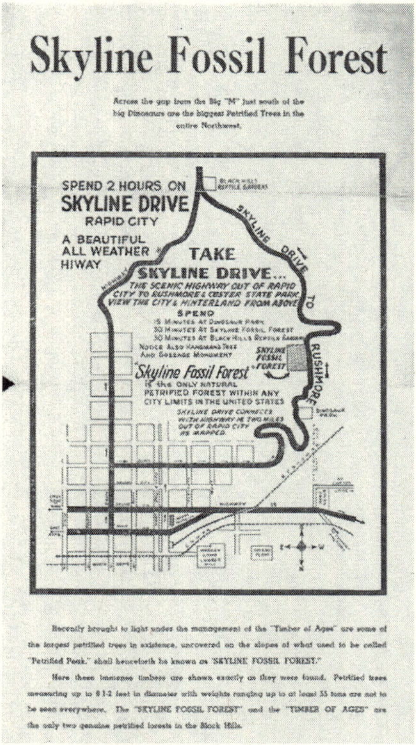


An ad for the various tourist attractions on Skyline Drive, 1930. *South Dakota State Historical Society*

the "Timber of Ages" petrified forest at Piedmont. To make the site more impressive, these men developed hiking trails and brought in more petrified wood, and Brockelsby added the log-shaped concession stand. Business, however, seldom met expectations. The Petrified Forest closed in the early 1960s, and the concession stand burned in 1965. Hiking trails still wind through the "forest," although little petrified wood remains. The foundations of the concession stand can still be seen at the edge of the parking lot.

**Rapid City Amphitheater:** West of the Petrified Forest are the remains of a large outdoor amphitheater. In 1934, New York newspaperman Kenneth Ellis began promoting a grandiose event he called the "Pageant of America." His proposal included a four-hour stage show, where representatives would highlight significant events from each state's history. Ellis saw the program as a natural complement to Mount Rushmore, and he estimated it would draw between 25,000 and 50,000 people a day for two months. He convinced local, state, and federal officials to lend their support. George Mansfield once again stepped forward and donated the hillside for the outdoor amphitheater, and the federal government approved $36,500 for the WPA to hire up to one hundred men to improve it. Everything seemed to be in motion for the July 1935 opening when suddenly the program was canceled for lack of money. Workers had already terraced benches into the hillside. The amphitheater hosted concerts in the 1940s, and evidence of its earthen benches still exists.

2.6 mi **Reptile Gardens' original location, junction of Skyline Drive and Tower Road:** Reptile Gardens, one of the Black Hills' premier roadside attractions, got its start at this location in 1937. Owner Earl Brockelsby broke into tourism by working as a guide at Hidden City, south of Rapid City, and at the Petrified Forest just east of this location. He would often include a rattlesnake as part of his routine, and he quickly realized that people were both terrified and fascinated by reptiles. These experiences motivated him to open a tourist attraction that featured snakes. The twenty-one-year-old entrepreneur borrowed money and built a white stucco structure with rattlesnake pits.

Brockelsby chose this location because it sat on US 16, the main route to Mount Rushmore, and because it was at the top of a steep hill. Many pre-war motorists, stopping to let their engines cool, found him there with a snake and a sales pitch. As visitation grew, Brockelsby brought in more exotic snakes and a small collection of other animals, such as coyotes and a black bear. Reptile Gardens closed when Brockelsby left for military service in 1943. The shuttered business fell into disrepair. When he returned two years later, he had to start over. He gave the building a brightly colored brick-and-stone façade, and he expanded his collection of animals to include 1,700 reptiles and a land tortoise named Methuselah, whom children delighted in riding. Reptile Gardens prospered but Brockelsby anticipated trouble when the highway department decided to relocate US 16 a quarter mile to the east. He lobbied against the change, to no avail. With his business less accessible, he decided to relocate to Spring Creek Valley, four miles south, in 1964.

2.6 mi **Turn right (south) onto Tower Road/US 16 Service Road. Travel south 0.5 miles to access US 16.**

3.2 mi **Turn right onto US 16. Follow US 16 to its intersection with US 16A at the Keystone WYE.**

**Roadside attractions:** Gutzon Borglum, the sculptor of Mount Rushmore, worried that roadside attractions would detract from his monument's grandeur and patriotic message. To keep the tourist shops as far away as possible, the federal government designated 1,300 acres of land as part of the memorial. Nonetheless, several roadside attractions sprang up at Keystone, just outside of Mount Rushmore's grounds, and along US 16. Just as Earl Brockelsby had recognized the advantages of opening Reptile Gardens on the main route to the mountain, several other creative entrepreneurs followed suit. Only a few of the more historic tourist attractions will be mentioned.

4.0 mi **Marine Life:** In 1963, as traffic to Mount Rushmore increased, two Rapid City businessmen, Joe Hrachovec and Guy Van Nice, opened Marine Life, one of the region's more unusual roadside attractions.

Hrachovec and Van Nice knew aquariums and marine animal shows were popular, and with none closer than a thousand miles, they anticipated drawing tourists from throughout the region. The pair found a favorable location, just two miles from Rapid City, and their attraction proved a success. The large seal statue in front of their building soon became a local landmark. Marine Life featured sea lions, penguins, and a variety of exotic fish, but the dolphin show probably attracted the most visitors. Hrachovec and Van Nice, however, ran into operating challenges. Since they had to care for the animals in the winter, they needed to either keep the facility open or ship them to marine attractions elsewhere in the country, generally in Florida—both expensive options. Then an illness swept through the facility in 1972, killing all the animals except for two seals. The attraction changed hands several times after Hrachovec and Van Nice sold in 1979. When new owners took over in 1995, they encountered high costs and hostile animal rights organizations and closed Marine Life in 1996. The animals went to an aquarium in China, and a small strip mall now occupies the location.

5.4 mi **Mystic Ranger District Office, intersection of US 16 and Moon Meadows Road:** In 2006 the federal government built the large Forest Service complex at the intersection to house the Mystic Ranger District office, the Forest & Grassland Research Laboratory, and the Forest Health Management office. Prior to its opening, two small offices served the Mystic District, one in Hill City and one in Rapid City.

**Black Hills National Forest:** President William McKinley used his executive authority to create the Black Hills Forest Reserve out of the region's public lands in 1897. Many locals protested the order and wanted the designation reversed, but their outcry only delayed it for one year, and the Black Hills Forest Reserve became a reality in 1898. It became the Black Hills National Forest when President Theodore Roosevelt transferred the forest reserves from the Department of the Interior to the Department of Agriculture in 1905. More administrative changes followed. For greater efficiency, President William H. Taft created two units in 1910, the Black Hills National Forest in the north and Harney National Forest in the south. President Dwight D. Eisenhower recombined the two forests under the Black Hills National Forest name in 1954.

The Black Hills National Forest is currently divided into four districts: the Bearlodge District has jurisdiction over the Black Hills within northern Wyoming and has an office in Sundance; the Northern Hills District oversees the northern Black Hills within South Dakota and has an office in Spearfish; the Mystic District controls the central Black Hills and has its office in Rapid City; and the Hell Canyon District covers the southern Black Hills, with offices in Custer and Newcastle.

5.7 mi **Fort Hays:** This tourist attraction capitalizes on the hit 1990 movie *Dances with Wolves*. Early in the film, the main character, played by Kevin Costner, reports to Fort Hays, Kansas. To stage that scene, Costner (who also directed and produced the movie) had a half-dozen buildings constructed near Caputa, east of Rapid City. Once filming wrapped, the landowner took possession of the structures and began offering tours, but the remote location limited visitation. Working with the landowner, Rapid City businessman Herman Jones moved the buildings next to US 16 in 1993 and opened the Headquarters and Supply House for tours. Jones then constructed other structures and shops, but the centerpiece of his attraction became the Fort Hays Chuckwagon Supper & Show.

In 2020, Jones and his son, Clint, added a rollercoaster known as the Buffalo Hunt Coaster. Riders shoot at plastic bison with laser-tag guns. This attraction seems to fall in line with the changes in tourism; either because visitors want more thrills and excitement than sightseeing can provide, or because attraction owners see thrill rides as an easier sell, such features as rollercoasters and zip lines have become more commonplace.

6.8 mi **Reptile Gardens:** After deciding to relocate in 1964, Earl Brockelsby bought forty acres of land in Spring Creek Valley for his new Reptile Gardens. To make it stand out, he built a translucent dome where he could create a tropical forest, replete with exotic birds and plants. Glass cages along the dome's interior walls held exotic snakes.

Earl Brockelsby, founder of Reptile Gardens.
*South Dakota Hall of Fame, Chamberlain, S.Dak.*

As he acquired more land Brockelsby added more attractions, such as Bewitched Village, where he placed a botanical garden and animal acts, including giant Galapagos tortoises that children could ride. When it opened in 1965, the new Reptile Gardens had become more than just another roadside attraction—it was a tourist destination unto itself.

Tragedy struck in 1976. The dome burned, killing thousands of reptiles and birds. Undaunted, Brockelsby regrouped and carried on. He built a new clear plastic dome, and he acquired a larger collection of snakes. In recent years, the staff has become increasingly concerned about humane treatment of the animals and ended the tortoise rides. They also have expanded their conservation and science education efforts.

7.0 mi **Spring Creek Valley:** Spring Creek starts in the southern Black Hills, flows into Sheridan Lake, then passes through this valley and out of the Black Hills just south of Rapid City. Prospectors searching the creek for gold found the yellow metal higher in the mountains, leading to the creation of Hill City and Sheridan. The mining history of those camps is covered more fully in the Gold Rush Tour.

9.0 mi **Bear Country U.S.A.:** A family trip to Yellowstone National Park in 1971 inspired Dennis ("Doc") Casey to establish Bear Country U.S.A. The Casey family spent several days in Yellowstone but saw only one bear. Not only did that frustrate Doc Casey, but that lone bear caused a major traffic jam as people stopped to look. The Rapid City dentist, realizing that people had a keen interest in wild animals, saw an opportunity to create a drive-through park where visitors could see animals in a natural setting. He called it Bear Country and opened in 1972 with fourteen black bears, one cougar, and one wolf. He soon added more animals, including mountain lions, elk, bison, and bighorn sheep. By 2000, Bear Country had about three hundred black bears and had become one of the most popular attractions on the road to Mount Rushmore.

Casey's death in 2000 set off a legal battle among his widow, Pauline, and their seven children over who would control Bear Country. The family split into two factions. At one point, Pauline called her family "dysfunctional." They finally reached a settlement in 2010: Pauline and three of the children took control of Bear Country, while two other children opened Bearizona in Williams, Arizona, just outside of Grand Canyon National Park.

9.8 mi **Sitting Bull Crystal Caverns:** To the south is Sitting Bull Road, named for a nearby tourist cave that operated from 1934 to 2015. Prospectors from Rockerville discovered the caverns in the 1880s, but with gold on their minds, they moved on. Several owners followed, mostly farmers and ranchers with no more interest in the cave than the miners. That changed when Rapid City businessman Alex Duhamel learned about the cave. Looking to capitalize on the growing tourist industry, he purchased it. While the cave is relatively small, it does contain some of the largest known calcite crystals, and Duhamel made those the centerpiece of his attraction. To increase the cave's appeal, he added his Sioux Indian Pageant, a program of American Indian dances and ceremonies created by Oglala Lakota

The ticket office tipi at the Sitting Bull Crystal Caverns, 1973. *Photo by Watson Parker, Watson Parker Ghost Town Notebooks, Leland D. Case Library for Western Historical Studies, Black Hills State University*

holy man Nicholas Black Elk, which Duhamel had been hosting at his Rapid City store since 1927. Black Elk is also credited with naming the cave to honor Sitting Bull, the famous Hunkpapa Lakota leader. To accommodate the pageant, Duhamel built a tipi-shaped ticket office, an octagonal dance hall, and a gift shop that he called the Trading Post. Sicangu Lakota artist Godfrey Broken Rope painted four murals depicting Black Hills scenes inside the dance hall. The pageant ended in 1957, but cave tours continued until 2015. According to a local newspaper, the property sold to a "developer."

Nicholas Black Elk is perhaps best known for his collaboration with author John G. Neihardt in the publication of *Black Elk Speaks* in 1932. The book provides a moving account of the importance of the Black Hills to the Lakotas. In 2016, the U.S. Board on Geographic Names renamed Harney Peak, South Dakota's highest mountain, in Black Elk's honor.

11.2 mi **Stratosphere Bowl, Stratobowl Rim Trailhead:** The parking area on the right (north) is at the trailhead for a path that leads to the upper rim of the Stratosphere Bowl. In the 1930s, the U.S. Army Air Corps and the National Geographic Society joined forces to explore the stratosphere with a manned balloon, but they needed a good location to stage the launch. The Rapid City Chamber of Commerce felt it could locate such a place and invited the selection committee to town. The group toured a few sites, including a flat meadow surrounded by high limestone walls known as Moonlight Valley. This location impressed the committee. Its 425-foot vertical walls provided protection against the wind, and it offered open prairie to the east of Rapid City where the balloon could land. To seal the deal, the chamber acquired the land and built a road to the site. Moonlight Valley became known as the "Stratobowl."

A hydrogen balloon lifted a three-man gondola known as Explorer I on 27 July 1934. After reaching just over 60,000 feet, the balloon split. As it lost altitude, the hydrogen exploded. The crew safely parachuted to earth while the gondola crashed into a Nebraska cornfield, resulting in a two-foot-high pile of debris.

Insurance money allowed the two agencies to try again. In July 1935, they planned to launch a balloon, filled with helium to eliminate

Explorer II lifts off from the Stratobowl on 11 November 1935.
*Photo by Lee Wells, South Dakota State Historical Society*

any chance of an explosion, and they developed a lighter two-man capsule known as Explorer II. As takeoff neared, the balloon sprang a leak, and the flight was canceled. The engineers tried again on 11 November. Thousands of people stood on the bowl's rim as the large balloon began ascending to an altitude of over 72,000 feet. The balloon and the crew then came to earth near White Lake, South Dakota,

230 miles east of the Stratobowl. They had been aloft for over eight hours and set a new world altitude record—for comparison, modern commercial airliners fly at between 31,000 and 42,000 feet. They had also performed several experiments, such as measuring ozone and cosmic rays, and gathered information that would prove valuable to later airplane flights.

The third and last balloon flight came twenty-one years later, in 1956, when two U.S. Navy pilots rode a skyhook balloon to an altitude of 76,000 feet. Despite this new balloon altitude record, planes had already reached 90,000 feet. Nevertheless, the flight collected information on how prolonged exposure to high altitudes affects human health.

12.2 mi **Rockerville:** The highway exit leads to the former gold camp of Rockerville, once a vibrant community and an important gold producer. Gold was discovered along this branch of Spring Creek in 1876, but a lack of water made it difficult to recover. Captain Jack Crawford, known as "The Poet Scout," was one of the early arrivals, and for a time the location was known as Captain Jack's Dry Diggin's. It was soon renamed Rockville or Rockerville, after the "rocker" or "rocker box," a piece of mining equipment that could recover gold using little water. Good results caused the town to prosper. Population estimates vary widely, but an 1879 count came up with 700 people. Contemporary Rapid City had 500.

**The Rockerville Flume:** To develop more efficient mining methods, the claim owners decided to bring in more water. Their plan called for taking water out of Spring Creek near Sheridan and transporting it with a flume to Rockerville. The project started in 1878 but quickly stalled. In 1880, Ambrose Bierce, later famous as a writer and journalist, finished the seventeen-mile flume at a cost of $300,000. The wooden flume worked well enough to allow for hydraulic mining, in which water pressure is used to wash away overburden and expose the gold. About $500,000 of gold was recovered. (A Forest Service pamphlet claims that $20 million was produced, a gross exaggeration.) Rockerville boomed, with nearly a thousand people living there in 1880. Management problems and leaks in the flume eventually caused the operation to fail, but its legacy lives on; the flume's path has been turned into one of the Black Hills' most popular hiking trails.

Miners abandoned Rockerville, but tourist travel along US 16 to Mount Rushmore brought renewed activity. A gas station opened by 1930, then as tourism increased after World War II, entrepreneurs recreated a gold camp, offering a variety of attractions, including a saloon, a stagecoach ride, and a melodrama. The tourist venue prospered until the highway department rerouted US 16 around the town in the late 1960s. Although it sat just below the highway, visitation plummeted and profits disappeared. The recreated gold town eventually closed, leaving only the restaurant. Today, a few homes and the Gaslight Dining Saloon keep the memory of Rockerville alive.

**Gold Mining Continues:** The Rockerville area still has gold, and recreational miners continue to look for it. In 2010, two men discovered what they called the Ice Box nugget, the Black Hills' largest undisputed gold nugget in existence. The Ice Box nugget is not pure gold, however; it weighs 5.27 ounces and has a gold content of 3.96 ounces. The Potato Creek Johnny nugget, on display at the Adams Museum in Deadwood, is larger, but some people claim that Johnny created it out of many smaller nuggets.

16.9 mi **Cosmos Road:** The road on the left (south) leads to the Cosmos Mystery Area, a tourist attraction that opened in 1953. Two California college students camped in the area in the early 1940s and reportedly discovered a location where the laws of nature seemed to be confused. For instance, balls appeared to roll uphill. One of them returned and opened the "Cosmos of the Black Hills."

Often referred to as a gravity house or mystery spot, this type of attraction began appearing when auto tourism boomed after World War II. In fact, a gravity house had opened near Santa Clara, where the student who opened the Cosmos Mystery Area attended college. A visit there may well have inspired him to open the Cosmos. While the promoters like to credit such things as "gravity faults" or "supernatural forces," gravity houses depend on optical illusions. The horizon is oftentimes obscured at these locations, and without a reliable reference point, visitors have a hard time judging when objects are perpendicular to the earth.

When Cosmos of the Black Hills opened, the *Rapid City Journal* called it the "zaniest tourist attraction to appear in the Black Hills." In spite of that (or perhaps because of it), the Cosmos developed into a "large and profitable business," according to the owner. His good fortune attracted imitators. Three more gravity houses opened in the Black Hills: Dizzyland, Gravity Hill, and Mystery Hill. Because of its location and effective marketing, the Cosmos is the only one that remains.

17.6 mi **At the intersection of US 16 and US 16A, take US 16A. Go under the Keystone WYE and turn toward Keystone.**

**Keystone WYE:** The interchange of US 16 and US 16A is known as the Keystone WYE. It features two crossed bridges. The top bridge is supported by six arching beams made of laminated lumber. When the South Dakota Department of Transportation widened the road in 1967–1968, the designers chose this aesthetically pleasing design to complement the natural environment. As construction advanced, a truck carrying three of the timber beams rolled over, potentially damaging them. Replacements were made and installed, while the damaged supports were repurposed to create a three-legged pyramid that once served as a welcome arch at the edge of Rapid City. When a motel and convenience store were built at that location in the mid-1990s, the arches were relocated to Sitting Bull Crystal Caverns.

18.9 mi **Powder House Lodge:** The lodge owner states that the Powder House name comes from a small log building that once stored blasting powder for the nearby Bismarck and Ida Florence Mines.

20.2 mi **Intersection of US 16A and SD 40 (Reed Street): Turn left at the stoplight onto Reed Street and travel into historic or "old" Keystone. A stop is recommended on the left-hand side of the road in front of the Keystone–Holy Terror Mine.**

20.8 mi **Recommended Stop in Old Keystone: Pull into the small dirt lot next to the "Rock Shed," in front of the ruins of the Keystone and Holy Terror Mines.**

**Keystone:** The town has two parts: historic "old Keystone" and the more recent tourist section. This part of the tour focuses on old Keystone.

When compared to other Black Hills gold towns, Keystone was a latecomer. It was founded in 1892, after prospectors discovered the Keystone Mine. Still, much happened in the area before it was founded, especially along Battle Creek, which flows through the old part of town, and Grizzly or Grizzly Bear Creek, which flows through new Keystone.

**Early Prospectors:** Prospectors searched for gold along Battle, Grizzly Bear, and Iron Creeks as early as 1875, and discovered small amounts in Battle Creek. In fact, Walter P. Jenney, of the 1875 Newton–Jenney Expedition, claimed to have pulled up a rose bush near Battle Creek and shaken fifty cents of gold from its roots. Some of these discoveries were made close to the plains, which meant Lakotas were close by. One story even tells of warriors firing on a group of miners as they gathered around a campfire. None were hurt, but a bullet passed through their frying pan, persuading them to leave.

**Hayward:** One group of miners established a camp on Battle Creek about five and a half miles below Keystone in November 1876, naming it after Charles Hayward, one of its members. The gold they found was deeply buried, and the shafts they dug to reach it occasionally flooded. At other times Battle Creek had too little water to run placer equipment. To solve these problems, the prospectors dammed the creek and ran the stored water through hydraulic mining equipment to wash away overburden and expose the gold. In 1878, two hydraulic companies formed, the Iron Creek Flume and Mining Company and the Battle Creek Flume and Mining Company. Reports of rich finds were just wishful thinking. Still, other companies followed. The Battle Creek Gravel Mining Company built dams and flumes in 1880, but it also failed to produce gold.

**Custer County Seat:** When the territorial legislature created Custer County, the newly appointed county commissioners selected Hayward as the county seat in April 1877. But as mining stalled and people left in 1878 and 1879, residents of Custer City wanted the county seat moved. The issue was placed on the 4 November 1879 ballot and Custer won. To ensure the county seat's permanence, Custer residents built a courthouse in 1881. A survey that same year showed that Hayward was actually in Pennington County, ending any chance of it reclaiming the county seat.

One story claims that Custer residents, anxious for the county seat, stole the records soon after the election. The thieves were quickly caught and forced to return the documents. Custer had to wait until the official transfer date. Tales such as this one are commonly told about county seat fights, which brings the veracity of this account into question.

**Hayward Today:** Hayward hung on for a few years after 1880. While the town no longer exists, it is home to Rushmore Cave. Miners reportedly discovered the cave while searching for a leak in one of their flumes in 1880, but they paid little attention to it. Local residents also showed little interest until some young people discovered previously unknown chambers in the 1920s. The owners then decided to open the cave for tours in 1927 and changed its name from Hayward Cave to Rushmore Cave to capitalize on the publicity surrounding the dedication and early work on Mount Rushmore. The current proprietors not only offer tours but have also added a zip line and a rollercoaster. These amusements seem to appeal to a new generation of tourists who want more excitement than can be found in the natural wonder of a cave.

**Harney:** The camp of Harney sat two miles below Keystone on Battle Creek. It was laid out in 1876 but abandoned by 1878. Its story is similar to Hayward's: water problems seemingly prevented the recovery of gold, if any existed. Entrepreneurs occasionally tried to recover it, or at least convinced gullible investors to spend money on trying. In 1881, a company known as Harney (or Harney Peak) Hydraulic began building a long flume. It was supposed to channel water from both Grizzly Bear and Battle Creeks in a trestle 700 feet long and 200 feet high, to be built toward Harney through where Keystone is today. The promoters' goal was to create enough water pressure to uncover gold for about six miles along Battle Creek. After a year and a half, the operators had little to show for their efforts, and the investors finally saw it as a fraud. Harney was again deserted. Today there are only a few homes in the area.

**Harney Peak Tin:** Tin mining brought significant activity to the Keystone area, primarily along Grizzly Bear or Grizzly Gulch, closer to new Keystone. It began in 1883 when A. J. Simmons sent a sample of ore from the Etta Mine to an expert, asking for a "determination." William Blake, a respected mining man, did the analysis in California, reporting over 75 percent metallic tin. Blake soon labeled the hill "Tin Mountain." This was a big deal as the United States had no paying quantities of tin and imported up to $24 million of the metal from Great Britain each year. Reports circulated that "these mines will certainly rule the tin market of the world." Simmons sold his interest to businesspeople in New York for what one paper called a "handsome consideration" in June 1884. The New York investors then organized the Harney Peak Tin Mining, Milling and Manufacturing Company.

The company began developing the mine and expanding its holdings. It bought claims throughout the area and built a mill near the Etta Mine in 1886. A small town known as Stanum sprang up. But as it transpired, Simmons had sold investors a tin mine with little tin. Whether he knew that is unclear. He had a good reputation and would later serve as mayor of Rapid City, but he was "always an optimist" and was involved in several mining enterprises, some of which turned out to be failures and possibly frauds.

After the initial failure, the owners proclaimed that the first results were not indicative of what existed. Other samples showed "admirable" returns and an important source of tin. The directors also began selling stock in London, with influential British investors joining the board of a reorganized company beginning in 1887. There were many critics of the company. The *Engineering and Mining Journal* speculated that it was reorganized so the New York shareholders could unload worthless stock. In any case, the new Harney Peak Tin Company bought more property. By 1892, it had 1,100 mining claims. With each claim representing a little over ten acres, it controlled about 11,000 acres of land, and the company went on a building spree. It refitted the Etta mill, constructed hoisting plants at its five principal mines, and built several new structures around Hill City, including a 250-ton mill, boardinghouses, blacksmith shops, carpenter shops, machine shops, an office, the Alpine Inn, a foundry, and storehouses. The monthly payroll reportedly totaled $30,000.

After operating for about two months, in February 1893 the Hill City mill shut down, with little tin recovered, putting 400 men out of work. The New York interests had indeed perpetrated a fraud. They had duped the London shareholders into investing an estimated $3 million in a company that produced only $1,545 worth of tin. The fiasco became internationally infamous.

The only positive outcome was the Alpine Inn. As the inn's website states, the company "spent millions of unseen investor's [sic] dollars boosting the town's economy," while encouraging the Burlington Railroad to build through Hill City in 1890.

**The founding of Keystone:** Although placer mining, flume building, and tin speculation occurred in the area, little development occurred along this section of Battle Creek, except for the construction of a few stores and cabins, until three prospectors staked the Keystone claim in 1891. One of them, Jacob Reed, also located the Reed Placer Claim along Battle Creek and platted the town of Keystone on his claim in 1892.

**Holy Terror:** Keystone began to prosper after William Franklin, known as Rocky Mountain Frank, accidentally discovered what would become the Holy Terror Mine in 1894. Many stories exist about the mine's discovery, but one version has Franklin and his daughter picking strawberries on the side of Mount Aetna, on Keystone's west side. While resting, something bright caught the young lady's eye. She called her father over, and he recognized gold. Franklin promptly staked a claim, naming it the Holy Terror, reportedly "honoring" his wife. It soon became, as a Department of the Interior publication states, "one of the most famous mines in the Black Hills."

Franklin and a partner dug a shaft and soon hit abundant high-grade, free-milling gold ore, which could be readily treated by available processes. In fact, gold could be seen protruding from the native quartz. The Holy Terror and the Homestake were about the only two mines in the Black Hills that had abundant free-milling ore; the Holy Terror ore was valued at $500 per ton. As Franklin and his partner brought in other investors, they built a small stamp mill and began producing $10,000 per week, which attracted national attention. After a year, they sold out. The new owners deepened the shaft and erected a larger mill. One author states that as gold production increased, the Holy Terror became the anchor of the southern Black Hills' economy and "brought dignity" to a region whose reputation had been damaged by the Harney Peak Tin scandal.

In 1898 the owners of the Holy Terror and the Keystone Mines consolidated operations, driving tunnels between the two properties. Reports claim that $570,000 in gold was produced in 1898–1899. The mines were forced to close in 1903. The troubles began when the shaft flooded and the company struggled to dewater it. Then an explosion and fire killed three miners and injured seventeen others. Litigation followed, with the company losing several expensive lawsuits. In the years after, the mine operated intermittently. A new mill went up in 1929, but it burned. Another was built in 1939, but the government ordered gold mines closed during World War II and it never reopened. The Holy Terror and Keystone Mines produced an estimated $1.3 million in gold.

**Bullion Mine:** The Bullion Mine sat just east of the Keystone–Holy Terror complex. It carried gold and silver, but it also contained sulfides and arsenides, making the ore difficult to treat and profits elusive. A boll weevil infestation in southern cotton fields reversed the Bullion's fortunes in 1924. With arsenic in demand, the mine owners sent ore to the Globe smelter in Denver for treatment. When the smelter successfully recovered nearly fifty tons of arsenic, the Bullion built a processing plant at the mine site. Just as the price of arsenic had gone up quickly, it went down quickly, and the plant soon closed. Efforts to recover gold also failed, and the mine was done by 1930.

**Other prospects:** Several claims were staked across the valley from the Holy Terror, but few prospered. The Columbia dug a 300-foot shaft and produced some gold from a small but seemingly rich vein. The Lucky Boy also had a 300-foot shaft but showed no results. Keystone's most famous mine may be the Big Thunder, which has been a heavily promoted tourist attraction since the 1960s. It is located on the Reed Placer Claim, the same claim as the town. Two German immigrants dug what was called the Krupp Tunnel at that location in 1892 or 1893, but there is no record of production.

**Pegmatite Mining:** The 1920s brought new mining activity to the area when prices for the minerals found in pegmatite ores went up. Mines such as the Peerless, the Hugo, and the Etta opened. Most of these were located closer to Grizzly Bear Creek, near new Keystone, but a feldspar-grinding plant was built along the railroad in 1928, near the junction of Grizzly Bear and Battle Creeks, just above old Keystone. It burned in 1957.

**Recent gold activity:** An advance in gold prices brought renewed attention to the Keystone area. In the 1990s, a company drilled sixty test holes, without going into production, and from 2012 to 2015, Mineral Mountain Mining signed an exploration agreement with the owners of the Holy Terror. This Toronto-based company bought several other claims. It drilled forty test holes but went no further. While the operators apparently found gold, they felt it was not practical to mine at the time. They could return if conditions become more favorable. After leaving Keystone, Mineral Mountain began exploring around Rochford in 2018.

**The Burlington Railroad:** The Burlington built into Keystone from Hill City to serve the Holy Terror, Keystone, and Bullion Mines in 1900. With the Holy Terror–Keystone closing in 1903, the spur had little traffic. Its main products became feldspar, beryllium, spodumene, and arsenic. The railroad continued operations on the branch until the 1972 Black Hills Flood severely damaged the track.

**1880 Train:** The Black Hills Central Railroad (BHCRR) began running excursions into Keystone when it changed from narrow gauge to standard gauge operations in 1965. After the 1972 flood destroyed the track, trains stopped at what was called Keystone Junction, a little distance from town on the Old Hill City Road. The BHCRR owners eventually reconstructed the line to Keystone to better capitalize on tourist traffic.

**Mount Rushmore:** When Gutzon Borglum selected nearby Mount Rushmore to carve his monument, Keystone residents recognized the potential benefits. To make sure their town sat on the path to the mountain, they used axes, shovels, and horse-drawn scrapers to open a "passable" road in time for Borglum's 1925 dedication. They also arranged to have horses and teamsters stationed along the route to help faltering automobiles. Locals may have also opened the first Rushmore-related concession when they sold barbecue elk sandwiches at the Congregational church. For lack of funding, little happened at the mountain until President Coolidge came to town for a 1927 dedication. The president's limousine stopped at a pool hall where he drank a bottle of soda. With western imagery in mind, he mounted a horse and led his entourage to Mount Rushmore. After Coolidge's visit, work on the monument began in earnest. Despite occasional shutdowns when funds ran out, between twenty-five and thirty former Keystone miners found work at the monument, and other Rushmore employees moved to town, finding plenty of empty houses to choose from. The old mining camp also served as the project's supply center. The railroad delivered supplies, and the Keystone Consolidated Mines, which controlled the Holy Terror, provided power.

**Keystone in Good Times and Bad:** During mining's heyday, the town was a vibrant community, with a population of around 2,000 in the 1890s. It had a variety of businesses, including a reported sixteen saloons. But as the mines closed and people left, only about 300 residents remained. The business district similarly disappeared, mainly from fires—four hit town between 1908 and 1937. Because of the losses, few historic structures remain. One exception is the old Keystone School on the slope of Mount Aetna. Built in 1899, it served as a school until 1988, with its athletic teams known as the "Dynamiters." It is now a museum. Another historic property is Halley's General Store. Dating from 1896, it is Keystone's oldest continuously operated business. The store's name comes from James Halley III, who purchased it in 1917. His grandfather, James Halley I, was a prominent Rapid City citizen, serving as mayor and bank president.

**Famous Resident, Caroline Ingalls Swanzey:** A younger sister of author Laura Ingalls Wilder, Caroline Ingalls Swanzey lived in Keystone for over three decades. In addition to proving up on a homesteading claim outside Topbar, South Dakota, she had mastered the newspaper trade. She arrived in Keystone in 1911 to manage the *Keystone Recorder*, owned by the news magnate E. L. Senn. She also worked for the *Hill City Star*. The following year she married David Swanzey and quit her job to care for his children and her blind sister, Mary. Swanzey had come to the area before Keystone existed and staked a placer claim on Grizzly Bear Creek, where the Roosevelt Inn is today located in new Keystone. Besides prospecting, he worked odd jobs. In 1885, he and another man guided New York attorney Charles Rushmore on his inspection of Harney Peak Tin Company properties. It was during this trip that Swanzey reportedly named Mount Rushmore after his client. When the Burlington built to town, Swanzey became a station agent. He died in 1938 at the age of eighty-three. Swanzey Street is named after him. After his death, Caroline remained in Keystone until she passed away in 1946.

**Famous Residents, The Bower Family Band:** The Bower Family Band was composed of John ("Cal") and Keziah ("Kizzie") Bower and their seven children (five girls and two boys). They had formed the brass band in 1884 while living in Vermillion, but moved to the Black Hills soon after, perhaps to be closer to their daughter Alice, who had married Joseph Gossage, the owner of the *Rapid City Journal*, in 1882. Family members established homesteads on Battle and French Creeks and started giving concerts around the Black Hills. In the years that followed, the children took jobs throughout the Black Hills, and some got married. Even so, the band still gathered to perform. When Cal moved to Keystone in 1895, during the Holy Terror

The Bower Family Band, 1888. Standing, left to right: Sidney, Nettie, Lulu, Rose, Mayo; seated, left to right: Alice, Laura, John, Keziah, Quinnie. *Adams Museum Collection, Deadwood History, Inc., Deadwood, S.Dak.*

boom, several children followed. This allowed them to perform until the mine closed and the family moved away. In 1961, the youngest daughter, Laura Bower Van Nuys, now married to a professor at the South Dakota School of Mines, wrote *The Family Band: From the Missouri to the Black Hills, 1881–1900*, which was later adapted into a 1968 Disney movie, *The One and Only, Genuine, Original Family Band.*

**Glendale:** The gold, tin, and pegmatite mining that took place in Keystone also occurred in Glendale, a mile south of the former gold camp of Harney on Iron Creek. Prospectors reportedly found gold in Iron Creek, but little came of it. Promoters talked of building a flume through the area, primarily to carry water to mining operations on Battle Creek. In the early 1880s a prospector found tin in what was called the Otho Mine. The Glendale Mining Company of Chicago bought the claims in 1889 and built a 150-ton mill. Like other mines in the area, it failed to produce tin, and closed by 1891. Another company took over in 1892 and unsuccessfully looked for gold. In 1913, the property was refurbished and a new mill was installed to process pegmatites such as beryl and feldspar. It ran intermittently over the years, lasting until 1939. Some of the buildings survived, and a couple of Keystone businesspeople eventually remodeled them for the Meeting the Need camp, which officially opened for people with disabilities in 2005.

# Part Five Mount Rushmore

Route Overview: Return to the stoplight at the intersection of SD 40 (Reed Street) and US 16A (Winter Street). Turn left at the intersection, to the southwest, onto US 16A. Travel through new Keystone to the junction of US 16A and SD 244. Turn right onto SD 244 to Mount Rushmore, where a stop is recommended.

Mileage starts at Keystone pullout.

0.0 mi **Lot in front of Keystone-Holy Terror Mine, downtown Keystone.**

0.6 mi **At the intersection of SD 40 (Reed Street) and US 16A (Winter Street), at the stoplight, turn left onto US 16A (Winter Street).**

0.6 mi **New Keystone:** Although the first businesses to capitalize on Mount Rushmore's fame opened in "old" Keystone, with the increase in tourism after World War II shops soon appeared along US 16A and Grizzly Creek, creating "new" Keystone. The expansion in tourist venues also brought a greater variety of enterprises, many of them reflecting the changing nature of tourism. The earliest establishments catered to travelers' basic needs, such as gasoline and food, but shop owners quickly realized that visitors wanted mementos of their visit. They responded by selling Mount Rushmore souvenirs. As traffic continued to grow, the merchants sought other goods that would appeal to tourists. American Indian–themed items seemed a natural fit for western South Dakota, and the "Indians" store opened in 1950. A taffy shop opened to cater to travelers who expected to find novelty foodstuffs in tourist towns. Stores that featured more traditional gifts, such as jewelry, soon followed. Recently, travelers have come to expect more than services and souvenirs. Some desire educational opportunities, while others want thrills and excitement. Entrepreneurs in new Keystone responded with the National Presidential Wax Museum, the Rushmore Borglum Story, and the Rushmore

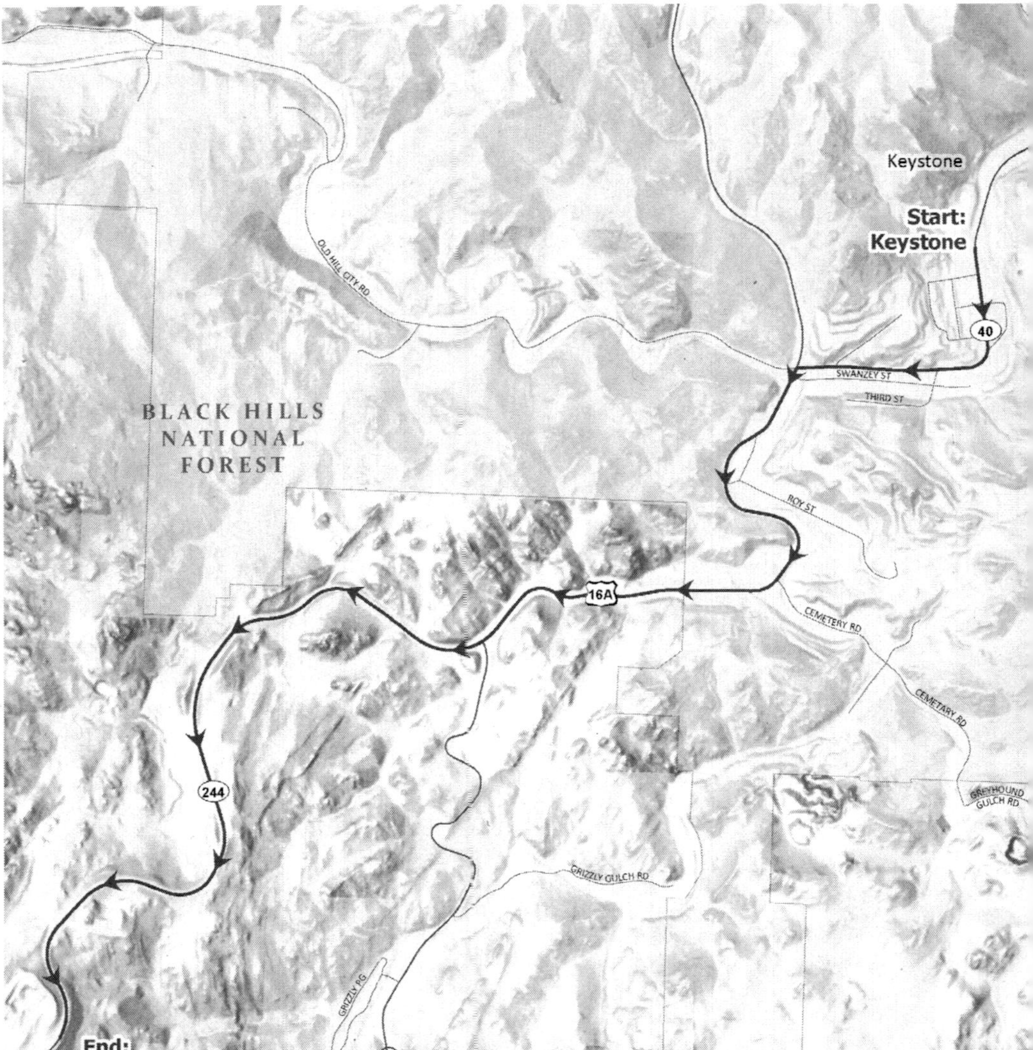
Keystone
Start:
Keystone
40
SWANZEY ST
THIRD ST
OLD HILL CITY RD
BLACK HILLS
NATIONAL
FOREST
ROY ST
16A
CEMETERY RD
CEMETARY RD
GREYHOUND
GULCH RD
244
GRIZZLY GULCH RD
GRIZZLY PG
End:
Mt. Rushmore
Esri, NASA, NGA, USGS, FEMA, South Dakota Department of Transportatic

"Alpine Slide." No matter what they sell, many business owners have given their stores a Western flavor by installing boardwalks and false fronts. Besides the usual challenges of running a seasonal tourist business, the owners have also had to deal with natural disasters. The Ruby House, for example, opened in 1970, offering food, antiques, and an old-timey atmosphere. The building was washed away in the 1972 Black Hills Flood and partially burned in a 2003 fire, but it was promptly rebuilt after each tragedy.

**1972 Flood:** The flood that brought devastation to Rapid City on 9 June 1972 also ravaged Keystone. Buildings on the east side of Winter Street disappeared, and half of the structures on the west side of the street suffered severe damage. Despite the disaster, most of the businesses reopened within a month.

1.0 mi **Peerless Mine:** The Peerless pegmatite mine can be seen on the hill behind the Roosevelt Inn. One of the region's more active pegmatite mines, it operated from 1924 into the 1950s. A successful Keystone businessman eventually bought the site and built the Keystone Project Ministry Center. Retreats for "discipleship training" are held there.

1.1 mi **The Etta Mine:** The Roosevelt Inn sits at the junction of Cemetery Road and Winter Street. The Etta Mine, the Etta Tin Mill, and Etta Camp, also known as Stanum, sat a little distance down Cemetery Road. They were associated with the Harney Peak Tin Company, which operated in this area from 1884 to 1889 and then moved to Hill City. After Harney Peak Tin left, the Etta Mine closed until new owners began mining pegmatites in 1898. The mine produced feldspar, mica, beryl, columbite-tantalite, and cassiterite, but it became famous for having some of the largest spodumene crystals ever found. Although Etta Camp also came back to life, gaining a few dozen people, Keystone had already become the region's dominant camp. After the Etta Mine closed in 1959, its workings remained accessible for a number of years. They have recently been fenced off. The Pacer Corporation, a company that produced feldspar and mica, purchased the property a few years ago but did little with it and has recently closed.

1.7 mi **Junction of SD 244 and Iron Mountain Road (US 16A). Turn right (west) onto SD 244 and toward Mount Rushmore.**

**Iron Mountain Road:** Though the tour leaves it at this point and follows SD 244 to Mount Rushmore, US 16A, or Iron Mountain Road, is famous for its pigtail bridges and scenic highlights. Senator and former governor Peter Norbeck, the moving force behind Custer State Park, wanted the road to enhance nature's beauty. Built in 1930–1932, it connects Custer State Park to Mount Rushmore. To better highlight Mount Rushmore, Norbeck put in three tunnels that frame the memorial. The road also has fourteen switchbacks and three pigtail bridges that curve the road over itself. The CCC built the picturesque bridges out of ponderosa pine logs. The road also has a section where the two driving lanes are separated. Norbeck hoped to give visitors the sensation of traveling on a forest path. In total, Iron Mountain Road succeeds in adding more adventure to a mountain drive. Changes have been made since it was originally constructed, such as steel I-beams supporting the bridges instead of logs, but the experience remains the same.

**Grizzly Creek campground:** About a mile up US 16A is Grizzly Creek campground. The CCC built the structures in a heavy rustic style featuring log and stone construction. The campground retains many of its original features.

Grizzly Creek picnic area, 2022. *Author photo*

2.9 mi **Mount Rushmore view, Gutzon Borglum marker:** This location offers a good view of Mount Rushmore.

3.2 mi **Recommended Stop at Mount Rushmore:** Stopping at Mount Rushmore allows for a better understanding of the monument, but there are other possible places to stop. There is a pullout where George Washington's face can be seen in profile, and there is a picnic area called Breezy Point a little distance from the memorial. While Breezy Point does not offer a view of the monument, it is a good place to take a break.

**Mount Rushmore:** As tourism became an important industry for South Dakota in the early twentieth century, state historian Doane Robinson wondered how to attract even more travelers, specifically to the Black Hills. He knew the visitors would give a much-needed boost to the state's economy, but he worried that they would quickly become bored with mountain scenery. He believed the region needed something special, and his thinking soon turned to mountain carving. Looking at the granite spires in Custer State Park's Needles, Robinson envisioned Lakota leaders, such as Red Cloud, and Western heroes, such as Lewis and Clark and Buffalo Bill Cody, carved into them.

With this concept in mind, Robinson needed a sculptor. After Lorado Taft declined his invitation, Robinson turned to Gutzon Borglum. Well known for his sculptures of Abraham Lincoln (one of which was displayed in the White House by Theodore Roosevelt), Borglum had become enamored with colossal art, which he saw as the best way to portray America's accomplishments. Borglum's first attempt at mountain carving was a commission by the United Daughters of the Confederacy to carve a Confederate memorial on the side of Stone Mountain in Georgia. They dismissed the sculptor before he completed the work, however; as Robinson would soon learn, Borglum's combative nature frequently antagonized people. Despite the problems in Georgia, Robinson invited the fifty-seven-year-old Borglum to the Black Hills in 1924.

Robinson came along just as Borglum's Stone Mountain project fell apart. He accepted the invitation, but quickly dismissed Robinson's ideas about carving Western heroes. Borglum instead saw a

Gutzon Borglum, sculptor of Mount Rushmore, ca. 1935. The incomplete monument in the background shows Jefferson's head in its original location, on Washington's right. *South Dakota State Historical Society*

chance to meld American art with patriotism and to do it on a grand scale. To accomplish that, he needed the proper site. With people protesting the use of the Needles, he looked elsewhere, ultimately identifying Mount Rushmore. It had the right size, location, and type of rock. Along with choosing the mountain, Borglum also selected the figures he would carve. George Washington and Abraham Lincoln, as the father of the nation and its savior, were guaranteed spots. He apparently chose Thomas Jefferson for his expansionist policies with the Louisiana Purchase. Theodore Roosevelt's selection, however, brought a protest from the late president's enemies. Borglum ignored the critics, arguing that Roosevelt should be honored for his assertive nationalism. Along with the four presidents, Borglum also planned to engrave a history of the United States on the mountainside in three-foot letters that he called an entablature.

Mount Rushmore was Borglum's project and design, but he often left the site, either to raise money or to do other artwork, leaving a foreman in charge. His biggest problem was the lack of funding. The

Mount Rushmore National Memorial Commission was formed to raise funds, with limited success. The financial problems frustrated Borglum, particularly that Black Hills residents did not contribute more. He often complained that they did not appreciate the great things he was doing for them. In the end, it took federal appropriations to complete the project. Senator Norbeck and South Dakota U.S. representative William Williamson gave the memorial their full support, which included gaining congressional backing.

Borglum had initially dedicated the monument in 1925, but nothing had happened afterward for lack of funding. All that changed when Borglum persuaded President Coolidge, who was vacationing in the Black Hills in the summer of 1927, to rededicate Mount Rushmore. On 10 August, the president put on cowboy boots and rode a horse from Keystone to Mount Rushmore. When he spoke, he stated that the people of South Dakota deserved "the sympathy and support of private beneficence and the national government." The project not only benefitted from the publicity, but also from Coolidge's apparent endorsement of federal backing. His statement greatly helped Norbeck and Williamson attract federal funding.

The first real carving began in October 1927 and lasted until the weather grew cold and the money ran out in December. By then, just a dent had been made in the mountain. Failure seemed probable, but then the federal money began arriving. The work, put on hiatus in 1928, resumed in 1929. Washington's head was completed and dedicated in July 1930. During that ceremony the mountain was labeled "The Shrine of Democracy," and Borglum famously declared, "Let us place there, carved high, as close to heaven as we can, the words of our leaders, their faces, to show posterity what manner of men they were. Then breathe a prayer that these records will endure until the wind and rain alone shall wear them away."

After the dedication, carving went on sporadically, depending on the funding. Jefferson's head presented a challenge. It was initially to be placed on Washington's right. Borglum had been away while the Jefferson head was being carved. When he returned, he saw that too much stone had been removed on the Jefferson head, and that there was not enough good stone for the Jefferson head anyway. He dynamited the unfinished head in 1934 and reconfigured the monument,

Gutzon Borglum (center, pointing), suspended next to Lincoln's head, undated. *Photo by Charles D'Emery, South Dakota State Historical Society*

moving Jefferson to Washington's left and shuffling the locations of Roosevelt and Lincoln.

The relocated Jefferson head was ready for dedication in 1936. President Franklin D. Roosevelt, touring the nation's Dust Bowl that summer, attended the ceremony and gave a brief speech. One year later, the Lincoln head was dedicated. The Roosevelt head followed in 1939, but there was still much work to do. For instance, Borglum had started the entablature in 1930, but had to use that space for the Lincoln head. With the entablature going by the wayside, Borglum decided to carve a Hall of Records. Envisioning it housing America's founding documents someday, he started drilling a cavern behind the monument but had to stop for lack of money in July 1939.

When Borglum died in March 1941, his son, Lincoln, took over the project and used the remaining budget of $50,000 to finish the Roosevelt and Lincoln heads and block out Jefferson's coat collar and Washington's coat collar and lapels. Borglum had originally intended to carve the figures to the waist, but that remained undone. The final drilling took place on 31 October 1941, and the workers dismantled the machinery in November 1941. Congress declared Mount Rushmore complete. No final dedication was held.

Overall, it took fourteen years to finish the monument, but the intermittent nature of the work meant that carving went on for only six and a half years. During that time, about four hundred men were employed on the mountain. Many of them came and went. Around twenty-four workers were there at any given time, but that number fluctuated depending on funding. In the end, Borglum and his employees removed about 450,000 tons of stone. The memorial cost $989,992.32 (around $20.5 million in 2024), which included Borglum's honorarium of $170,000. The federal government contributed about 85 percent of the total bill.

**Modern Visitor Center:** The construction of a new visitor center and gift shop caused some controversy in the 1990s. The previous facilities had been built in the 1950s and included rustic features such as stonework and wooden beams, which seemed to fit in the natural setting. When visitors viewed Mount Rushmore from the observation decks, they could easily take in the surrounding Black Hills. Locals believed that Borglum would have approved of the design, and they were dismayed when the National Park Service replaced the old facilities with a visitor center and a multi-story parking garage that seemed straight out of Washington, D.C. They felt the new complex corrupted the mountain setting and Borglum's vision. When standing on the current viewing terraces, visitors can barely see the Black Hills. Another point of contention is the parking fee. When Congress appropriated money for the carving, it stipulated that there would never be an admissions charge. While that is still technically true, visitors must pay to park.

**Ben Black Elk:** Sometimes known as the "Fifth Face of Mount Rushmore," Benjamin Black Elk became nearly as famous as the four presidents. Born in 1899, he was the son of Oglala Lakota holy man Nicholas Black Elk, the namesake of Black Elk Peak and a maternal cousin of Crazy Horse. After briefly attending Carlisle Indian Industrial School, Ben Black Elk became a successful rancher. He wanted

Benjamin Black Elk, sometimes called "the Fifth Face of Mount Rushmore."
*South Dakota State Historical Society*

to help preserve Lakota culture, however, and consequently served as an interpreter for John Neihardt when the author interviewed Ben's father for the book *Black Elk Speaks*. Believing it would help introduce people to American Indians, beginning in the 1950s Ben spent twenty years posing for photographs at the memorial, with as many as five thousand taken of him each day. He died in 1973.

**Protestors, AIM:** Mount Rushmore's fame has made it an attractive site for protesters, such as the American Indian Movement (AIM). Taking inspiration from the Civil Rights movement, Dennis Banks and Clyde Bellecourt founded AIM in 1968 to have a unified voice when fighting for Indian issues. One of its more famous actions was the occupation of Alcatraz Island from 1969 to 1971.

Just as the occupation of Alcatraz was coming to an end, AIM organized an occupation of Mount Rushmore. On 6 June, twenty AIM members (eleven women and nine men) led by Russell Means of the Pine Ridge Indian Reservation climbed the mountain and set up camp on top. They demanded that the United States uphold the Fort Laramie Treaty of 1868, which would mean returning the Black Hills to the Lakotas. After a twelve-hour standoff, park rangers removed the protestors and charged them with trespassing.

**Greenpeace:** Greenpeace is an international organization dedicated to using peaceful protest to expose global environmental problems. In 2009, eleven Greenpeace activists decided to challenge the Obama administration on its environmental policies. While eight of them blocked park rangers, the other three suspended a banner measuring sixty-five feet by thirty-five feet that said, "America Honors Leaders, Not Politicians, who Stop Global Warming" to the right of Lincoln's head. The rangers quickly arrested the eleven protestors and took down the banner.

## Part Six Sylvan Lake and Custer

Route Overview: Travel southwest on SD 244 to its junction with Palmer Creek Road. Turn onto Palmer Creek Road and follow it to the junction with SD 87. Take SD 87 to Sylvan Lake Lodge. Just beyond the lodge, take SD 89 toward Custer. At the intersection of SD 89 and US 16A, turn right (west) onto US 16A. Follow US 16A to Custer's Way Park for a Recommended Stop.

Mileage starts at entrance to Mount Rushmore.

0.0 mi **Mount Rushmore entrance, Rapid City.**

0.7 mi **George Washington profile:** A small parking lot is available.

1.9 mi **Breezy Point Picnic Ground:** A pull-off on the right side of the road (to the south) leads to the Breezy Point picnic area. It provides an opportunity for a break in a forested setting. Part of the picnic ground sits on an early road to Mount Rushmore.

2.7 mi **Horse Thief Lake:** The CCC built a dam across Pine Creek in what was called Horse Thief Park in 1934. The South Dakota Game, Fish and Parks Department wanted the lake to provide recreational opportunities; since it sits on a road to Mount Rushmore, it has succeeded admirably. The neighboring campgrounds are consistently filled during the summers. In 2015 the state drained the eighteen-acre lake to remove silt. The accumulation was a normal occurrence as reservoirs generally collect the dirt their tributaries carry.

The valley was called Horse Thief Park because stage robbers and horse thieves supposedly rendezvoused there. A story in a 1935 issue of the *Lead Daily Call* claimed that Lame Johnny's gang buried loot in the area from "many" Cheyenne–Deadwood stage robberies.

**Lame Johnny:** The outlaw Lame Johnny is probably more famous than he deserves to be. Stories have him involved in just about every major stagecoach holdup in the Black Hills. He did steal horses, rob

Start:
Mt. Rushmore
BLACK HILLS
NATIONAL
FOREST
244
16
16A
87
89
OLD HILL CITY RD
PALMER CREEK RD
JEPSEN DR
JADE PL
SILVER TIP RD
Sylvan Lake Lodge
CAMP REMINGTON RD
IRON CREEK HORSE CAMP
AMERICA CENTER RD
CAMP BOB MARSHALL RD
CROOK ST
1881 Courthouse
Way Park
End:
Way Park
Custer
Gordon Stockade
Esri, NASA, NGA, USGS, FEMA, South Dakota Department of Transportation

a post office, and hold up at least one stagecoach, but every masked robber with a limp was alleged to be Lame Johnny. Regardless of how many crimes he committed, vigilantes eventually caught up with Johnny and hanged him near what is now known as Lame Johnny Creek, in the southern Black Hills, in 1879.

**Outlaw Hideouts:** Horse thieves and robbers allegedly had hideouts and rendezvous points, labeled "robbers' roosts," throughout the Black Hills. No doubt some of these locations just look like good hiding places to people who romanticize the Wild West and dream of buried loot.

5.9 mi **Palmer Gulch/KOA:** Troy Parker developed Palmer Gulch Lodge, the first tourist attraction at this location, in 1927. He built cabins, a lodge, and a golf course to entertain people who stayed a week or more in the Black Hills. A horseback ride to the top of Black Elk Peak was one of the highlights. The Parker family sold the facility in 1962, and

Tourists enjoy the view at Palmer Gulch Lodge, 1952.
*South Dakota State Historical Society*

the new owners turned it into a dude ranch. Recreational Adventures Co. bought it in 1972, first franchising it as a Holiday Inn Travel Park and then as a KOA in 1977. By offering a variety of camping options and amenities, including the traditional horseback rides to Black Elk Peak, it has become one of the largest KOAs in the world.

6.2 mi **Turn left (west) onto Palmer Creek Road, FS Road 350:** The graveled Palmer Creek Road leaves the "beaten path" and provides interesting views of Black Elk Peak, Palmer Gulch, and the surrounding country. Prospectors found small amounts of gold in Palmer Gulch during the early days of the gold rush and named the creek and gulch after one of their comrades. John Brennan prospected Palmer Gulch in the winter of 1875–1876 but grew tired of the cold and hard work and left in February 1876. With a few associates, he ventured to the eastern slope of the Black Hills and established Rapid City, hoping to create a "Denver of the Black Hills." Although Brennan gave up on Palmer Gulch, other prospectors continued to look for gold. Evidence of their work remains.

Palmer Creek Road was designed to highlight the Black Hills' natural beauty. It includes a section where the route divides and travels through a split rock that frames Black Elk Peak.

6.7 mi **Split Rock, View of Black Elk Peak:** When automobile tourism first became prominent, road designers were mindful of offering scenic views and interesting drives. By featuring Black Elk Peak, the split rock drive is an example of this thinking. At one time, a sign to the right of the rock formation noted that Harney Peak, as it was then known, was the highest peak east of the Rocky Mountains, at 7,242 feet.

**Black Elk Peak:** While leading a topographical survey of the Black Hills in 1857, Lieutenant Gouverneur K. Warren named the peak after General William S. Harney, his superior officer. Warren and his command mostly stayed on the plains as they traveled around the Black Hills and only saw the peak at a distance. Harney's reputation for brutality led the U.S. Board on Geographic Names to rename the mountain in honor of Nicholas Black Elk in 2016.

A fire lookout tower can be seen on the top. The Forest Service built a small cabin for a fire lookout in 1911. The wooden structure was enlarged over the years, but the CCC eventually replaced it with the existing stone tower in 1939. It stopped serving as a fire lookout sometime around 1967 but remains a popular destination for hikers.

7.3 mi **The Palmer Creek Trailhead:** This trailhead leads to hiking and horseback riding trails that go into the Black Elk Wilderness area.

9.1 mi **Intersection of Palmer Creek Road and SD 87: Turn left (south) onto SD 87 toward Sylvan Lake Lodge.**

**Highway SD 87:** The trip to Sylvan Lake Lodge highlights the granite spires that are part of the crystalline or central core of the Black Hills. These are the oldest and hardest rock formations in the Black Hills. Since they erode more slowly than the neighboring sedimentary formations, they have become quite rugged. Black Elk Peak, Mount Rushmore, and the Needles are part of the central core.

12.7 mi **Sylvan Lake Lodge and Custer State Park:** A South Dakota State Parks pass is required to visit Sylvan Lake Lodge and Sylvan Lake. If you have a pass, a stop at either location is worthwhile. If you do not have a pass, take a quick look as you drive by the lodge and then follow SD 87 to where it meets SD 89 for the trip to Custer. Daily and annual park entrance licenses can be purchased online from South Dakota Game, Fish and Parks at gfp.sd.gov/pel/.

**Peter Norbeck:** A native of Redfield, South Dakota, Peter Norbeck entered politics after he had established a successful well-drilling business. He was elected to the state legislature in 1908 and soon advanced to the governor's office and then to the U.S. Senate, where he served from 1921 until his death in 1936. As a progressive Republican, he believed that government should make life better for South Dakotans and successfully advanced state loan and hail insurance programs to help struggling farmers. Custer State Park grew out of his desire to protect the Black Hills' scenic beauty while also making it accessible to the public. He fully appreciated how tourism could help the state's economy. In fact, he had no qualms about manipulating or enhancing the natural setting to make it more appealing to tourists, and his work in the Black Hills, from creating roads in Custer State Park to supporting Mount Rushmore, is a testament to his vision.

**Custer State Park:** After first visiting the Black Hills in 1905, Norbeck soon began promoting the idea of establishing a state game preserve in the region. His dream got a big boost when South Dakota's congressional delegation asked Congress to consolidate state school sections in the southern Black Hills. When South Dakota became a

Peter Norbeck (standing) at the State Game Lodge, 1927. The man waving his hat might be "Dakota Clyde" Jones, Black Hills riding instructor for President Calvin Coolidge. *South Dakota State Historical Society*

state, the federal government granted it sections 16 and 36 in each township for the maintenance of schools. Since that included several timbered sections within the National Forest, the state found the scattered land holdings difficult to manage. Congress agreed to the swap, and the state received a block of over 60,000 acres in 1912. State officials had to figure out what to do with the land. They initially designated it as a state forest and held timber sales to raise money. At Norbeck's urging, the legislature created a state game preserve in 1913. To make sure the transplanted bison, antelope, elk, and other animals stayed in the preserve, the state fenced it in, with Norbeck personally supervising the work. The state, in essence, had created a drive-through wildlife park.

Once in the governor's office, Norbeck pushed to make the game preserve a full-fledged state park. The legislature supported his vision and created a park board to manage it in 1919. Norbeck would be a leading voice on the board for years. He now saw commercial logging as hurting the park's natural beauty and gradually had it curtailed. He also wanted to provide more camping and lodging facilities, so the state constructed what would become known as the State Game Lodge in 1920. The building burned soon after it opened, but a new lodge quickly replaced it.

The original 60,000 acres did not include the scenic areas around the Needles, Sylvan Lake, and Black Elk Peak. Norbeck consequently persuaded a South Dakota congressman to sponsor a bill that would place 30,000 more acres of federal land under state control. Congress and President Woodrow Wilson agreed in 1920. There were a couple of contingencies, however. While the state may have been given control of the 30,000 acres, the federal government retained ownership and could take it back. Additionally, Norbeck wanted Sylvan Lake and the hotel as part of the park, but they were privately owned. He persuaded a special session of the state legislature to appropriate $50,000 to purchase the 200 acres that included the lake and the hotel. More additions made it the largest state park in the United States at 127,000 acres. A sizable portion of the additional land was designated as the Custer State Park Game Sanctuary. The federal government eventually took control of the sanctuary and removed 56,000 acres from the state park, including Black Elk Peak, to create the Norbeck Wildlife Preserve in 1949. This action left Custer State Park at its current size of 71,000 acres, no longer the largest state park in the country but still in the top ten.

**Sylvan Lake:** Theodore Reder created Sylvan Lake in 1891–1892, making it the first significant reservoir within the Black Hills. Reder, a Rapid City sawmill owner, builder, and developer, came across a small stream in Sunday Gulch that flowed through a gap in a rock wall and realized that he could create a lake and a possible tourist attraction without too much difficulty. The timing seemed right; the Burlington Railroad had reached Custer in 1890, and it would hopefully bring in pleasure seekers. Reder bought mineral claims to acquire the land, filled the gap in the rock formation with concrete, and created a ten-acre body of water he called Custer Lake. A friend's wife came up with Sylvan Lake, referencing the area's beauty and seclusion. (Sylvan, from the Latin *silva* or *sylva*, meaning "wood" or "forest," is defined as a shady wooded area, a restful setting. A silviculturist is a person who grows trees.)

**Sylvan Lake Hotel:** In 1892, with the dam complete, Reder built a three-and-a-half-story, sixty-six-room hotel, with a dining room,

The original Sylvan Lake Hotel, in an undated postcard by the O'Neill Photo Company. *South Dakota State Historical Society*

along the lake's south shore, as well as a wagon road to Custer and a trail to the top of Harney (Black Elk) Peak. Even so, the business struggled, probably due to the seven-mile wagon ride to reach the lake from Custer. Reder sold it to Joseph Spencer in 1896, who leased it to a series of operators. As roads and transportation improved, the resort gradually became more popular. Peter Norbeck, recognizing the setting's beauty and the resort's value early on, added it to Custer State Park in 1920.

**Sylvan Lake Lodge:** The Sylvan Lake Hotel burned in June 1935. The Custer State Park Board knew the hotel needed to be rebuilt, but it could not agree on a location or an architect. Norbeck thought that Frank Lloyd Wright could design a hotel that would bring an artistic element to the park and attract more visitors (during his career, Wright would design more than a thousand public, commercial, and residential buildings). Wright expressed interest in the project and even visited the park to select a location. He favored an area in the rocks behind the former hotel. The other board members, however, saw the hotel as a business proposition and believed people would only care about how much the rooms cost, not the aesthetic quality of the building. The businesspeople prevailed and hired South Dakota architect Harold Spitznagel to plan the new hotel. Spitznagel had previously designed the park's museum and would adhere to the more traditional park aesthetic of a wood-and-rock exterior—something Wright surely would not have done. The business element on the board also wanted more parking and easier accessibility, and they decided to locate the new hotel a little distance from the lake. The project received money from the Public Works Administration (PWA) and workers from the WPA and the CCC. The WPA did much of the work on the lodge, while the CCC built cabins, the store, and the water system. The new hotel opened in the fall of 1937. Spitznagel's final design did not incorporate logs, which were commonly utilized in park buildings, but the lodge still had a rustic appeal, with native pine boards and pegmatite rocks used as siding. A rear terrace provides a view of the lake and Black Elk Peak.

**Winter recreation:** To extend the tourist season, Custer State Park officials and tourism boosters tried to promote winter recreation at Sylvan Lake. Ice skating, ski racing, and toboggan rides were started in the 1920s, but a drive to develop other activities came in the 1930s. In 1932 the Black Hills Commercial Club adopted the slogan, "Get the Black Hills in the Minds of the People Twelve Months a Year," meaning more winter sports. The Black Hills Winter Sports Club took the charge seriously and developed the Black Hills' first ski jumps, one for professionals and another for less skilled skiers, on Silver Tip Peak, just across from the hotel. The larger jump allowed skiers to be airborne for two hundred feet. The Winter Sports Club saw the Sylvan Lake area as ideal for hosting annual winter carnivals, but lack of snow dampened the enthusiasm for winter sports.

**Modern tourism:** As Sylvan Lake and the hike to Black Elk Peak have become increasingly popular over the years, the influx of visitors has nearly overwhelmed the area. Proposed solutions have included limiting visitation, requiring reservations, and developing more parking lots.

13.1 mi **Junction of SD 87 and SD 89: Turn right (south) onto SD 89 for the trip to Custer.**

**Needles Highway:** SD 87 enters Custer State Park via the Needles Highway. To make the park's beauty accessible, Norbeck wanted a road through the granite spires known as the Needles. Together with state engineer Scovel Johnson, he laid out the route by horseback, procured supplies to build it, and supervised construction. It was a difficult job, requiring the labor of 165 men. When the road opened in late 1921, people marveled at its tunnels and wonderful vistas. Needles Highway quickly became a popular route and remains one today. Although not included in this tour, the highway is part of Peter Norbeck's legacy.

19.0 mi **Intersection of SD 89 and US 16A. While the tour turns right (west) toward Custer, there is an optional portion to the east.**

**Tour option: The reconstructed Gordon Stockade and several interpretative signs that deal with the origins of the Black Hills Gold Rush are two and a half miles east of the SD 89 and US 16A intersection on US 16A. This information is also covered in the Gold Rush Tour.**

**The Custer Expedition and the Origin of the Gold Rush:** The Black Hills Gold Rush started in this valley, and many explorers, gold seekers, and visitors ventured through it. In the summer of 1874, the U.S. Army dispatched Lieutenant Colonel George A. Custer to the Black Hills to find a suitable location for an army post on the western edge of the Sioux Indian Reservation, later called the Great Sioux Reservation. Custer commanded over one thousand soldiers, including a geologist, a topographer, and a regimental band. Sixty-three American Indian scouts assisted the troop, including Custer's aide, Bloody Knife. A number of civilians also came along, such as reporters from three national newspapers, two gold prospectors (Horatio Ross and William McKay), an African American cook (Sarah "Aunt Sally" Campbell), and a photographer (William Illingworth). Leaving Fort Abraham Lincoln near Bismarck, North Dakota, the Custer Expedition crossed the plains to the western side of the Black Hills, traveled past Inyan Kara Mountain, and entered the Black Hills near what is today Buckhorn, Wyoming, on 25 July. Five days later, the column arrived at French Creek. After briefly camping where the town of Custer is today, the entourage moved on and set up what was called Permanent Camp about two miles east of this intersection. The Custer troop camped there from 1–5 August. Prospectors Ross and McKay discovered gold along French Creek on 2 August. While they had detected a small amount of gold a few days earlier, they uncovered enough at this location to send a wave of excitement through the camp, and several other people from the expedition joined them in looking for gold. On the next day, Custer led a group of men to the Cheyenne River, about forty miles to the south. From there, he dispatched a scout named Charley Reynolds for Ft. Laramie, carrying news of gold in the Black Hills. Newspapers quickly spread the story across the country, and the Black Hills Gold Rush was on.

**The Early Gold Rush and the Government Response:** With the nation mired in an economic recession since the Panic of 1873, many people wanted their share of the Black Hills' riches. Exploration and gold mining companies quickly formed in several communities, such as Cheyenne and Bismarck, with the hope of venturing to the Black Hills. The 1868 Fort Laramie Treaty, however, forbade non-government employees from entering the Sioux Indian Reservation, which included all of South Dakota west of the Missouri River. The army issued warnings to stay away and sent patrols to remove any trespassers. Two Sioux City, Iowa, promoters named Thomas Russell and Charles Collins refused to be deterred and organized an expedition that became known as the Gordon Party, named after the troop's captain, John Gordon. It comprised twenty-six men and one woman, Annie Tallent, who joined her husband, David, and their nine-year-old son, Robert. The Gordon Party left Sioux City on 6 October and successfully evaded army patrols as they traveled westward. Once in the Black Hills, they followed Custer's trail to what was known as Custer's Gulch on French Creek, arriving on 23 December 1874. There they built a square stockade, measuring eighty feet on each side, by driving thirteen-foot poles three feet in the ground. They added bastions at the corners and cut loopholes every six feet along the walls. They also constructed seven cabins inside, three along each sidewall and one opposite the gate, and dug a well, uncovering small amounts of gold. They completed their work on 16 January 1875.

As the winter progressed, the ground froze, making prospecting difficult. Still, they managed to dig several holes, finding "colors" in most. Overall, life proved uneventful, with Mrs. Tallent re-reading the two books that she brought. In February, Gordon and another party member, Eph Witcher, left to recruit more gold seekers and obtain supplies. Over the next few weeks, six more bored and lonely men left for Ft. Laramie. Their meager discoveries notwithstanding, the men told exaggerated stories of gold, and the excitement spread.

The army soon found out about the interlopers and sent a patrol to remove them, but severe winter weather drove it back to Ft. Laramie. The army then conscripted two of the former camp members to lead another patrol in late March 1875. With more moderate weather and knowledgeable guides, it arrived at the stockade on 5 April. The commander gave the remaining people two days to cache their tools and lay out a townsite, which they named Harney City before they moved out. Once at Ft. Laramie, they were set free.

Since the stockade sat on French Creek, near the first discovery of gold, it became the focus of early gold seekers and a landmark for Black Hills travelers. When the government sent geologists Henry Newton and Walter Jenney, along with fifteen assistants and four hundred soldiers under Lieutenant Colonel Richard Dodge, into the Black Hills to determine the region's value in the summer of 1875, the expedition camped within four hundred yards of the stockade, close to if not on the same land where Custer had camped the year before. The Newton–Jenney Expedition called it Camp Harney and made the stockade their supply depot.

Other visitors included General George R. Crook, who made two stops at the stockade. He first came to the Black Hills with around a hundred men to remove miners who had illegally slipped into the region in early July 1875. Oddly, Crook and Dodge were working at cross purposes. Crook was attempting to uphold the 1868 Fort Laramie Treaty, while Dodge was ensuring the safety of scientists who were determining if enough value existed to violate that treaty and annex the Black Hills. As Crook prepared to leave the Black Hills with upwards of five hundred trespassing miners, he and Dodge rendezvoused near the stockade on 27 July. Crook put Dodge in charge of removing miners, but Captain Edwin Pollock would soon take over that duty.

Crook, or at least his command, would again pass by the stockade a year later, in the fall of 1876. After the Battle of Slim Buttes, fought north of the Black Hills against the Miniconjou Lakotas led by Crazy Horse and American Horse, Crook's two thousand men marched to the Black Hills to resupply. Desperately short of food, the trip challenged the men's endurance and became known as the Starvation or Horsemeat March, as the men resorted to eating their horses and mules. In the northern Black Hills, Crook left his troops under the command of Colonel Wesley Merritt, who led them through the Hills to French Creek, where they camped from late September into October on the same ground the Custer Expedition had used two years before.

When the gold rush ended, the stockade became a forgotten relic and fell into disrepair. Several efforts to rebuild it over the decades culminated in the current stockade, built in 2005 at a cost of $825,000 of state and federal money.

**Sidney Park Road:** About a half mile east of this location is Sidney Park Road, named after the Sidney-to-Custer Trail. From Sidney, Nebraska, the trail passed through Camp (later Fort) Robinson and entered the Black Hills through Buffalo Gap, along Beaver Creek. After swinging around Point of Rocks, a large outcropping near Pringle, the trail ran north, entering French Creek Valley near today's Sidney Park Road. This route was heavily traveled during the gold rush's early days, but when Deadwood became the focus of the excitement, most of the Sidney traffic bypassed the Buffalo Gap–Beaver Creek–Custer route and went up the east edge of the Black Hills, going through Rapid City, Crook City, and on to Deadwood.

19.0 mi **Return to main portion of the tour: Go west from intersection of SD 89 and US 16A to Custer.**

19.6 mi **Custer YMCA:** Two blocks south of the intersection of US 16A (Mt. Rushmore Road) and 7th Street, and barely visible from the road, is a large log structure at 644 Crook Street. The Custer Women's Civic Club saw a need for a recreation and community center and spearheaded the construction of this building. The group hired Berge Berglund, a Norwegian log worker, to build the fifty-by-one-hundred-foot structure, and persuaded Grace Coolidge to dedicate it in 1927—by happenstance, President Coolidge and his wife were spending that summer in Custer State Park. Known as the Custer Community Center or the Grace Coolidge Memorial Log Building, it houses Custer's YMCA today.

**Custer's First Jail:** A small stone structure labeled Custer's First Jail sits in front of the community center. An informational sign states that it originally sat across the street and that its first occupant was Wilber Todd, the person who built it. He apparently spent his pay on alcohol, got drunk, and was arrested.

President and First Lady Coolidge, ca. 1927. *Photo by Ralph Russell Doubleday, South Dakota State Historical Society*

**Custer Business District:** The blocks that run from 7th to 4th Streets on US 16A (Mt. Rushmore Road) are the center of Custer's business district. While primarily targeted at the tourist trade, there are several structures that highlight Custer's history.

**Kleemann House (1883), 619 Mt. Rushmore Road:** Paul Kleemann built the prominent two-story brick structure on the right-hand (north) side of the street. A native of Germany, Kleemann came to the Black Hills in 1877. He tried mining at Hayward and Rockerville before arriving in Custer in 1880. Although he continued to dabble in mining, he entered the hotel business and built this namesake property in 1883. The main floor had five rooms, including a bar and a dining room, and the upstairs was divided into nine bedrooms. Kleemann promoted it as the "only first-class hotel in town," and he apparently entertained such guests as Buffalo Bill Cody. Kleemann operated the hotel until his death in 1902. Family members took control and eventually sold it. A succession of owners gave the facility a variety of names, including Pine Cone Inn and General Custer Motor Lodge. The old building fell into disrepair by the late twentieth century, and the city condemned it in 1991. New owners came to the rescue in 2010, elegantly restoring and remodeling it into an upscale vacation rental that opened in 2012.

With the hotel's restoration, Kleemann's legacy lives on in Custer. At the time of his death, he was praised for his work on behalf of the city and county, but he was also described as blunt and outspoken, earning him both friends and enemies. The *Custer Chronicle* described him as "rough at times" but with a kind and generous heart.

**First National Bank of Dakota Territory (1911), 588 Mt. Rushmore Road:** On the southwest corner of the intersection of Mt. Rushmore Road and 6th Street is a sandstone commercial structure built for the First National Bank in 1911. The bank opened in 1881 and moved into a wood-frame building on this corner in 1883. This building replaced it. Its heavy stonework and rectangular windows resemble several sandstone structures built in the Black Hills in the late nineteenth and early twentieth centuries.

**"The Heidepriem Co." (1910), 538 Mt. Rushmore Road:** In 1910 Fred Heidepriem built the large two-story brick building with "The Heidepriem Co." painted across its top. Heidepriem, a Black Hills pioneer, walked from Cheyenne to Custer in August 1876. He searched for gold in the area around Sunday Gulch, near today's Sylvan Lake, finding four nuggets but little else. He joined the rush to Deadwood Gulch, but with the diggings already overcrowded, he worked as a carpenter and cabinetmaker instead and reportedly built the first frame dwelling in Lead City. Looking for a stable income, he returned to Custer and went into the construction and furniture business. He built Custer's first schoolhouse and then opened a small store in 1879. There he made all types of furniture, including caskets, and he soon became an undertaker.

As business grew, Heidepriem had this commercial structure built. While he focused on woodworking and undertaking, his wife and children ran the store. By the time of his death in 1917, Heidepriem's two sons, Fred and Eric, had taken over the business. They continued to run Heidepriem Furniture until 1959. When they closed, local newspapers called it the oldest family-operated business in the Black Hills. While running the store, the Heidepriem family also became community leaders; one son served in the state legislature, and a daughter wrote the script for the Gold Discovery Days pageant. Custer residents performed the pageant annually as part of a community celebration in the early twentieth century.

**Garlock Building (1890), 522 Mt. Rushmore Road:** The Garlock Building is just down the block from the Heidepriem building. Thomas ("T. V.") Van Garlock arrived in Custer in 1884 and joined A. T. Van Devort in the hardware, machinery, and mine supply business. Garlock took sole ownership of the enterprise in 1886 and built this brick Commercial-style structure in 1890. Its decorative cornices, arched upstairs windows, and attractive façade led the Custer newspaper to describe the Italianate-designed building as the most elegant ever erected in Custer. Garlock changed his business over the years. He started with a hardware store, then converted it to a general mercantile, and finally opened an automobile agency. He became interested in cars early on, and when he purchased a single-seat model

Garlock's opera house in Custer, 2022. *Author photo*

in 1901, he was credited with having the first automobile in the Black Hills, if not the state. Garlock also became involved in banking and city government. To provide a place for meetings and entertainment he built an opera house in 1894. By the time of his death in 1920, he was described as one of the best known and well-liked Custer County residents. The Garlock Building has housed a variety of businesses since Garlock's passing, including a saloon. Today it is home to the *Custer Chronicle*.

**"Oldest Saloon in the Black Hills," 508 Mt. Rushmore Road:** In front of the Gold Pan Saloon on the south side of the street is a sign that says it is the "Oldest Saloon in the Black Hills." Such claims are hard to verify, but since Custer was the first town established during the gold rush, it could be true.

**"Historic Site," 541 Mt. Rushmore Road:** Over the door of Baker's Bakery & Cafe, the bright pink building on the north side of the street, is a sign that says, "Historic Site." It goes on to state, "Site of Saloon Where James Fowler (Alias Fly Speck Billy) Murdered Abe Barnes in February 1881. Billy was hanged by a mob." The event mentioned on the sign did occur in Custer and is discussed at an upcoming stop. It is difficult, however, to determine if this is the actual location. Not many years ago, Custer entrepreneurs featured this affair in a small show and tourist business known as Fly Speck Billy Trading Post. A dummy was suspended by a hangman's rope from the trading post's sign. This location once housed a bar and could have been where Billy killed Barnes. But it may also have been chosen randomly.

19.8 mi **Intersection of US 16A (Mt. Rushmore Road) and US 385 at stoplight: Continue west for one block.**

19.9 mi **1881 Courthouse, 411 Mt. Rushmore Road:** The two-story sandstone courthouse was constructed soon after Custer became the county seat in 1881. The tall windows, decorative brickwork, and prominent cornice reflect its Italianate design. Several Black Hills buildings built between 1880 and 1910 have similar features. Two wings that were added in 1915 have the same basic design, but with less ornamentation. The county constructed a new courthouse in the 1970s, and this city landmark was converted into a museum.

**Courthouse encounter:** The old courthouse was the scene of the infamous Custer Courthouse Riot in 1973. The trouble began in January of that year when Darald Schmitz, a white man, wounded Wesley Bad Heart Bull, a Lakota, in what was described as a violent barroom brawl in Buffalo Gap. Bad Heart Bull died en route to the hospital. Schmitz was arrested and charged with manslaughter. Outraged at what they believed was a lenient charge, around 200 American Indians, including several American Indian Movement (AIM) members, planned to protest during the preliminary hearing. As the authorities prevented AIM supporters from entering the courthouse, a police officer knocked down the dead man's mother and a riot erupted. Around twenty people gained entrance to the building, but others wrecked police cruisers and set fire to cars, the chamber of commerce building, two gas stations, and the courthouse. The police arrested thirty people. The riot changed little, and Schmitz was later convicted of manslaughter. Bad Heart Bull's death, along with the earlier killing of Raymond Yellow Thunder in Gordon, Nebraska, are often cited as catalysts for the occupation of Wounded Knee.

**Wounded Knee II:** Later that month, around 250 American Indians occupied the hamlet of Wounded Knee, site of the 1890 massacre, to protest a variety of injustices. The immediate cause was a political dispute between traditionalists and the reservation government led by Pine Ridge tribal chairman Dick Wilson, who had recently evaded impeachment on numerous charges including corruption and nepotism. A seventy-one-day armed standoff began on 27 February 1973, when U.S. Marshals, FBI agents, and Bureau of Indian Affairs (BIA) representatives blocked roads and besieged the occupiers. Two of the occupiers were killed; fourteen more were wounded, as well as one U.S. Marshal. The standoff ended on 8 May when the Nixon administration agreed to discuss treaty rights, but the talks brought little change. Wounded Knee has been a controversial topic ever since, especially as it gained international attention and left many Lakotas divided between supporting AIM and resenting its presence on the reservation.

19.9 mi **Recommended Stop in Downtown Custer: Way Park, 424 Mt. Rushmore Road, the courtyard of the County Courthouse, opposite the 1881 Courthouse.**

**Way Park:** This park is named for Henry Way. A noted Custer citizen and county judge, Way donated the park and cabin to the city.

**The Flick Cabin:** The City of Custer's website gives this narrative about the log cabin: "The Dr. Flick cabin was the first building erected in the Black Hills. Dr. D. W. Flick built it of substantial hand-hewn logs and designed it as a home for his family." It is difficult to verify this account. Dr. Daniel Flick arrived early in the gold rush, and several sources credit him with building one of the first cabins in Custer. But it is unknown if it was the first cabin in the Black Hills, which seems unlikely. Henry Way identified this log building as Custer's first cabin in 1923, nearly fifty years after the gold rush. Way also placed the Shankland family in the cabin, not Dr. Flick. The structure does date from Custer's early days, although it is not in its original location. Way had it moved from where it once stood, where the gold discovery monument now stands.

Despite the uncertain early history, an apocryphal story has been told about the cabin. It states that Flick started building the cabin in August 1875, but he left it unfinished when General Crook removed him and the other trespassing miners. Captain Pollock supposedly finished the cabin and used it as his headquarters when he took over guarding the Black Hills. After he departed, Captain Jack Crawford took up residence there. When Flick returned in April 1876, he insisted the cabin was his and threw Crawford's belongings into the street. The two men took their dispute to a miners' court, where the jury ruled in Flick's favor. He used it as a residence and an office until he left for Rapid City around 1880. The Flick–Crawford dispute may well have happened, but no evidence of it can be found in the historical record.

**Horatio Ross Memorial & Gold Discovery Monument:** The stone tower with the gold pan on top was meant to recognize the first discovery of gold and the person who discovered it, but two things stand out. First, Horatio Ross and William McKay, members of the Custer Expedition, are generally credited as the discoverers of gold, but the memorial credits only Ross, probably because he lived in Custer until his 1904 death at the age of sixty-six and is buried in the Custer cemetery. The second issue is the listed discovery date of 27 July. When Ross was called upon to relate the story of discovery, he may have used that date, but the expedition was camped on Castle Creek, near a stream called Gold Run Creek, on 27 July. There is a report that McKay uncovered small amounts of gold there, but no other evidence exists. It is much more widely accepted that the first significant gold discovery happened on French Creek, close to Custer's Permanent Camp, on 2 August. These discrepancies aside, the monument's tower highlights a variety of local rocks and minerals, including rose quartz and petrified wood.

**The Monument's Creation and Gold Discovery Days:** By the early 1920s, Black Hills pioneers and area commercial clubs had become interested in highlighting the region's past. Whereas the pioneers wanted to celebrate their generation's achievements, the commercial clubs saw an opportunity to promote tourism. No matter the motivation, the Custer Business Men's Club led the charge in building the Ross gold discovery monument in 1921. The group collected money and hired stonemason Monte Nystrom to erect the stone tower out of donated rock specimens. They set the dedication for 27 July, mistakenly believing that was the anniversary of Ross's gold discovery, and they also erred in claiming that Ross had made that discovery only a few blocks from the monument's site. Regardless, the dedication was part of a "Pioneer Day" celebration that included a parade, a barbecue, a baseball game, speeches, band music, and other festivities. With thousands of people from throughout the Black Hills attending, the occasion's success inspired the Custer Women's Civic Club to start the Gold Discovery Days Pageant in 1922, a four-part event with performances depicting the "creation of the universe," "Lakota culture," "discovery of gold," and "growth of Custer City." The pageant soon morphed into a three-day rodeo, but it was discontinued in the 1950s. It has recently been resurrected as a summer celebration with a carnival, a car show, an arts & crafts fair, volleyball, a 5k run, hot-air balloon rides, and a parade.

**Custer City's founding:** Custer City got its start when General Crook was removing miners from the Black Hills in 1875. With Crook's approval, miners met on 10 August, just before their forced departure, to found Custer City. They formed a town-site company, laid out the town, divided it into lots, and ran a lottery to distribute them. Custer City replaced a town called Stonewall City that had been laid out a month earlier. A few miners began building cabins in Custer City, but development came to an abrupt halt as most left with Crook. The general allowed a few men to stay behind to guard the tools and belongings that the departing prospectors left at the site.

**Army removal and boom:** When Captain Pollock assumed responsibility for removing the miners, he took a harsher stand than Crook. After establishing his headquarters in Custer, he and his troops searched the Black Hills for trespassers. He confined the captured men to an outdoor jail called a "bull-pen" that sat just west of Way Park. He then sent them under guard to Ft. Laramie. By fall 1875, the army had worked to uphold the 1868 Fort Laramie Treaty for almost a year, but President Ulysses S. Grant was under political pressure to open the Black Hills to miners and settlers. Recognizing the futility of keeping the prospectors out, Grant gave up and ordered the troops withdrawn in late 1875. Gold seekers rushed in as Pollock and his troops left, bringing Custer to life. One entrepreneur brought a steam-powered sawmill, and nearly 100 rough-cut houses and a small number of businesses soon appeared. A Cheyenne newspaper described Custer City as a "lively" place with 500 or 600 people by February 1876, and it quickly grew to a population of a few thousand. Custer was the Black Hills' first town.

**Sidney and Cheyenne Trails:** The two most important trails to the Black Hills, the Sidney Trail from the east and the Cheyenne Trail from the west, converged in Custer. The Cheyenne Trail entered the Black Hills through Red Canyon, which starts just north of Edgemont, and followed Pleasant Valley to a location about four miles west of Custer, now called Fourmile. The trail then turned toward town. The town's status as a crossroads meant that most gold seekers, no matter their ultimate destination, came to Custer in the early days of the rush and helped it boom. To handle the wagon traffic, the town founders created a wide Main Street to allow bull teams to turn in the road. Unlike most mining towns, Custer's valley location offered plenty of room. Once in town, prospectors who wished to head north could choose from a couple of trails. One left town close to today's US 385, and another went up French Creek.

**Violence in Custer:** Custer experienced all the problems of a gold rush boomtown, which naturally included violence. Clashes with American Indians were very pronounced in the camp's early days. The camp was readily accessible from the neighboring plains, allowing gold seekers and their Lakota pursuers to enter easily. The warriors wanted to keep the interlopers out, but also to take their horses. One observer estimated that Lakota warriors killed twelve whites on the outskirts of town or on nearby roads in one month in 1876. The ongoing threat spurred Custer's residents to form militia units. Captain Jack Crawford led one group of 125 men known as the Custer Minutemen, but they proved ineffective at deterring violence. Within the camp itself, residents sometimes turned to guns to settle their differences. Ironically, the first killing was an accident: In late February 1876 two partners got drunk and started taking turns shooting at a bucket. One was killed by an errant bullet. A miners' court quickly tried the perpetrator. Since the shooting was accidental, the jury found him innocent of murder, but guilty of shooting firearms in town, which resulted in a thirty-dollar fine.

This killing was followed by what one chronicler called the "first authenticated" Black Hills murder. In March 1876, C. C. Clayton, described as an "all-around desperado," shot a one-time mail carrier named Boueyer, claiming he had stolen his horses. A miners' court found Clayton guilty and wanted him hanged. The judge instead recognized that the court had no legal standing and ordered him banished from camp. As the prospectors moved on and the population plunged, the chances for gunplay quickly diminished. Gold camps, no matter their size, still had moments of violence, and Custer was no exception. In 1881, James Fowler, known as Fly Speck Billy, invited Abe Barnes to have a drink with him. When Barnes refused, the drunken Billy shot and killed him. The sheriff arrested Billy, but a local vigilante committee intervened and hanged him. A Deadwood paper put it more delicately when it said Billy died from a "sudden pressure to his windpipe."

**From Boom to Bust:** Custer's boom proved brief. The gold was sparse and difficult to recover. Part of the problem came from French Creek's limited water and lazy flow. Miners liked substantial water and a good current to operate their sluice boxes. They also found few quartz outcroppings that carried gold. Many soon left, either for home or for new diggings in the north, especially when stories of great finds in Deadwood Gulch filtered through the Black Hills in the spring of 1876. Custer City was all but deserted. One observer counted only fourteen residents remaining. The trails still came through, however, providing opportunities to sell supplies, and the grassy valleys encouraged small cattle ranches to open. More importantly, some miners found only frustration in Deadwood and returned to rework old claims for previously overlooked gold ore outcroppings—a pattern that repeated itself throughout the Black Hills. By 1880, Custer's population had stabilized around 300.

Developments in the 1880s helped guarantee Custer's permanence. The residents successfully persuaded Custer County voters to move the county seat from Hayward to Custer, leading to the construction of the impressive 1881 courthouse. The discovery of tin ore northeast of Black Elk Peak in 1883 brought further growth, especially as English investors took charge of what was called the Harney Peak Tin Company, buying hundreds of claims and creating a new boom. The arrival of the Burlington & Missouri River Railroad in 1890 seemingly guaranteed economic security. The rail connection allowed for mica mines to open, commercial timber harvests to expand, and tourism to begin, at least in small ways, causing the town's population to more than double.

**Pegmatite Mines:** After the initial rush to Custer had ended, gold played only a minor role in the town's future. Instead of gold, miners sought minerals known as pegmatites, crystals that contain industrial or rare earth minerals such as mica, feldspar, and spodumene (lithium). Chemically identical to the host granite, pegmatite crystals form when a portion of the igneous fluids cool more slowly than the neighboring rock. Feldspar has been used in fire retardants, caulks, sealants, glass, ceramic tile, glazes, and bricks; mica in oil and water drilling, sound dampening, insulation, and paints; and spodumene in lubricants and medicine. In the Black Hills, pegmatites are generally found around Black Elk Peak, near Custer, and in the northwestern Black Hills near the Wyoming border. The pegmatite mines in the Custer area have most frequently produced mica and feldspar. To the west of town are two of the more famous pegmatite mines because of the minerals found there: the Tin Mountain Mine and the Tip Top Mine. Black Hills mineralogist Tom Loomis writes that 250 mineral species are found in the Black Hills, twenty-two of them new to science, and the Tip Top Mine accounts for the majority of these.

Much like gold mining, pegmatite mines had periods of boom and bust. Successful pegmatite mining depended on demand and price, which varied widely over the years. For instance, the early electrical industry used mica for its insulating qualities, causing several mines to open, but other products replaced it in the early twentieth century. When cassiterite, a type of tin ore, was identified, it caused a frenzy of speculation, bringing significant development to Keystone and Hill City between 1883 and 1893. In the end, the extent and value of the tin ore was limited. Feldspar was the most important pegmatite in the 1920s and 1930s, with several mines and processing plants opening. It is still mined today. Most pegmatite operations were modest, with miners digging small open pit and underground workings to access the minerals. Reminders of these activities still exist, from abandoned mines to the names of roads.

**Pacer Corp.:** The Pacer Corporation operated a feldspar plant just west of Custer until its recent closing. Consolidated Feldspar built the original mill in the 1920s. After it burned in 1958, International Minerals rebuilt it, and Pacer Corp. acquired it in 1972. Established in 1970, Pacer Corp. also mined and processed mica. After a 2018 change in ownership, the company bought more mines, including the Etta and the Tin Mountain, and updated its processes, but it seems that was insufficient for the company to survive.

**Custer Today:** The county and federal governments are important year-round employers in Custer. The U.S. Forest Service has its Black Hills headquarters here. Summer tourism also adds a big boost to the economy, with Custer State Park, Wind Cave, Jewel Cave, and Crazy Horse Memorial nearby. The streets of Custer are filled with visitors in the summer but are quiet in the winter.

## Part Seven Hill City

Route Overview: From Way Park travel one block east to the intersection with the stoplight. Turn left (north) on US 16/385 and travel to Hill City. Once at Hill City, take the bypass and turn into the Mickelson Trailhead in Tracy Park for a Recommended Stop.

Mileage starts at Way Park.

0.0 mi **Way Park, Rapid City. Turn right (east) onto Mt. Rushmore Road, US 16/385.**

0.1 mi **Intersection at stoplight: Turn left (north) on US 16/385. Custer Expedition:** Custer and his column of over one thousand people entered and left French Creek Valley on a trail that sits near US 385. The expedition came into the valley from the west, intersecting with US 385's eventual route just outside of town. Leaving town, Custer followed the same path before angling to the west farther up the hill, about where Medicine Mountain Road connects with US 385. In both directions, the expedition would have had a good view of Thunderhead Mountain, which is now Crazy Horse Memorial.

1.0 mi **U.S. Forest Service's Black Hills Headquarters:** In 1905, when President Theodore Roosevelt transferred the nation's forest reserves from the Department of the Interior to the Department of Agriculture, they became National Forests. The original Black Hills National Forest encompassed much of what is in the forest today, but it has gone through several administrative changes. President William H. Taft divided the forest into two units in 1910. The northern section took the Black Hills National Forest name and was headquartered in Deadwood. The southern section became Harney National Forest, with its office in Custer. While the change was made for more effective management, in 1954 President Dwight D. Eisenhower recombined the forests for better efficiency, with Custer chosen as the headquarters. This office complex was built in 1971–1972.

End:
Tracy Park
Hill City
Start:
Way Park
Custer
BLACK HILLS
NATIONAL
FOREST
Tracy Park
Poplar St
16
16B
16A
87
89
Esri, NASA, NGA, USGS, FEMA, South Dakota Department of Transportation

4.5 mi **Crazy Horse Memorial:** The inspiration for this carving began with Oglala Lakota chief Henry Standing Bear, a maternal cousin of Crazy Horse. Partly motivated by the work on Mount Rushmore, he saw a mountain carving as a way to preserve his people's culture and history. After visiting with various sculptors, including Rushmore's Gutzon Borglum, Standing Bear turned to Korczak Ziolkowski, who had worked for Borglum during the summer of 1939. A self-taught and relatively inexperienced sculptor from New England, Ziolkowski gained fame by winning a first-place medal at the 1939 New York

Korczak Ziolkowski, sculptor of Crazy Horse Monument. *South Dakota State Historical Society*

World's Fair. Standing Bear told Ziolkowski that a sculpture would bring hope and reconciliation to his people, and that it should be in the Black Hills, a place sacred to the Lakotas. Ziolkowski agreed to come to the Black Hills in 1947 and soon after accepted the challenge. He and Standing Bear selected Thunderhead Mountain, with Ziolkowski gaining control of it by staking mining claims. He made drawings and models of the proposed carving and dedicated the project in 1948. For the next thirty-four years, Ziolkowski made slow progress on the memorial. With his family's help, he also developed a visitor center, a museum, a business, and a home, and dreamed of building a university and a medical school. When he died in 1982, he was laid to rest in a tomb at the base of the memorial. Today the complex includes the Indian Museum of North America, the Native American Educational and Cultural Center, and the Indian University of North America.

**Ruth Ziolkowski:** When Ziolkowski came to the Black Hills he was married to Dorothy Comstock. She came from a prominent New England family, and the couple had a daughter, Ann. Not long after arriving in the Black Hills, they divorced. She claimed mental cruelty. In 1950 Ziolkowski married Ruth Ross, a student from New England who had followed him west to volunteer at the memorial in 1947. They had ten children together, five boys and five girls. Ruth handled many of the day-to-day operations, from running a timber mill, a dairy farm, and a gift shop, to overseeing improvements. She took over the Crazy Horse Memorial project upon Korczak's death. Ruth passed away in 2014. Some of the children and several grandchildren remain involved. After Ruth passed away, the Crazy Horse Foundation Board appointed Laurie Becvar as the memorial's

Ruth Ziolkowski. *South Dakota State Historical Society*

CEO. The choice surprised some, as she came from outside the family and organization. After several years at the helm, Becvar left the memorial project. Whitney Rencountre II was selected as CEO in 2022.

**Odds and ends:** The people at the Crazy Horse Memorial take pride in the fact that they have never accepted federal aid, partly because they do not want federal oversight. There are some ironies with the project. First, no known image of Crazy Horse exists. The design was Ziolkowski's best guess. Second, some Lakotas see dynamiting the mountain as violating the Black Hills' sacredness.

**Mickelson Trail:** This hiking and biking trail is visible just east of US 385 immediately after the turn into Crazy Horse Memorial. The trail sits on the Burlington Railroad bed that was built in 1890. The Burlington used the line until 1983. Soon after its abandonment, South Dakota Game, Fish and Parks officials began discussing turning the railroad right-of-way into a trail. The idea sat dormant until the Burlington began pulling up track and dismantling trestles in 1985. Recognizing that the cost of replacing trestles might end any chance of developing a trail, Guy Edwards, a Rapid City businessman, began organizing a grassroots effort to save the trestles and create a trail. Helping his cause was the 1983 National Trails System Act. The federal government passed this law to slow what seemed to be a dramatic loss of rail lines during the 1980s. It stated that inactive roadbeds could be preserved in a "railbank," with the hope that they would be returned to rail use in the future. In the interim, the roadbed could be used as a trail. Edwards also gained support from National Rails to Trails, a private organization that originated in the 1960s. By the time Edwards began promoting a Black Hills trail, the national group had successfully converted 21,000 miles of former railroad beds into trails.

Edwards organized a local rails-to-trails committee and quickly sought an agency that would take control of the roadbed and develop a trail. He ran into several roadblocks. Prior to the railbank law, abandoned railroad rights-of-way traditionally reverted to neighboring property owners, and while most of the rail line ran through National Forest land, the handful of private landowners along the route filed a

Aerial view of the fall foliage along Castle Creek, southwest of Mystic, 1974. On the right is the Rochford–Mystic Road; the railroad bed, on the left, became part of the Mickelson Trail. *Photo by C. E. Ferweda, Black Hills National Forest Historical Collection*

lawsuit attempting to stop it and acquire the land, delaying the trail's development until 1990. The Forest Service also proved unsupportive. When Edwards asked the agency to take control and make trail improvements, the Black Hills Forest supervisor refused, stating that he wished to avoid financial obligations and liability issues. This decision frustrated Edwards, and he later reported that the supervisor was uncooperative, even refusing to attend public meetings.

These obstacles could have killed the trail, but Edwards found supporters who kept it alive. While South Dakota Game, Fish and Parks had already expressed an interest in creating a trail, George S. Mickelson proved invaluable. During his campaign for the South Dakota governorship in 1986, Mickelson pledged to support the trail and have the state take control of the right-of-way. Once elected, he was true to his word. The state became the lead agency, working with the Burlington to transfer the right-of-way, defending the trail in court, and finding money to improve the route. Most importantly, Governors Mickelson and William Janklow directed hundreds of thousands of federal dollars to its construction under the 1991 Intermodal Surface Transportation Efficiency Act.

Once the South Dakota Supreme Court upheld a decision that allowed the state to take control of the right-of-way in 1990, actual construction began. Still, Edwards and others had to work diligently to find the money and manpower to improve the route. They sought private donations, which helped immensely, but several agencies were also crucial. Troops from the South Dakota National Guard rebuilt bridges, inmates from the Department of Corrections put up fences, and members of the South Dakota Mining Association volunteered their time. Also, a new Black Hills Forest supervisor reversed his predecessor's earlier stand and made the Forest Service a full-fledged partner, providing millions of dollars to build sections of the trail and rehabilitate four tunnels. Initial trail plans focused on the section from Hill City to Deadwood, but as the idea of establishing a trail developed, the state gained control of the entire branch line. The Burlington donated the section from Custer to Hill City to the state in 1988 and sold the Edgemont-to-Custer portion for $25,000 in 1990.

As work progressed throughout the 1990s, which included replacing nearly fifty trestles between Mystic and Deadwood, trail sections gradually opened. Governor Mickelson dedicated the first six miles in 1991, with more sections added in the years that followed. The 109-mile trail was completed in 1998 at an estimated cost of $5 million. It was initially called the Black Hills Burlington Northern Heritage Trail, but when Governor Mickelson and seven others were tragically killed in a plane crash in April 1993, it was renamed in his honor. For the trail to become a reality, key people, including Guy Edwards,

Governor Mickelson, and Dave Snyder, worked long hours over many years. According to state park official Doug Hofer, Snyder's financial support and leadership in attracting other donations was critical to the trail's completion.

8.9 mi **Oreville Campground:** The Oreville name comes from an 1890 station on the Burlington Railroad. The railroad saw this location as a potential shipping point for tin and other pegmatite ores. Despite several mines opening and the construction of a small beryllium refining mill, Oreville never grew beyond a few residents. Today, Oreville is remembered with a campground and a Mickelson Trail rest shelter.

9.7 mi **Black Elk Peak View:** The trip north on US 385 offers a good view of Black Elk Peak.

13.3 mi **Take the Hill City US 16 Bypass/Truck route.**

13.5 mi **Turn right onto Poplar Street to reach the Mickelson Trailhead.**

13.6 mi **Charlotte Tracy Park, Mickelson Trailhead, Recommended Stop.**

**Charlotte Tracy Park Cabin:** Bill Tracy built this cabin in Allen Gulch about half a mile west of Hill City around 1890. It was later moved to this location and is called the oldest remaining building in Hill City, which may or may not be true. The park is named after Tracy's daughter.

**Hill City History:** Hill City, also known as Hillyo and Hilltown, is the second oldest community in the Black Hills. Gold was discovered along Spring Creek in late December 1875, quickly attracting 500 people, 250 houses, two stores, and a hotel. Like Custer, it boomed for a few months and then most of the residents rushed north to Deadwood Gulch. According to legend, only an old man and a dog remained. A small resurgence occurred in 1877 as miners returned to look for hardrock claims. They produced enough gold to keep Hill

City alive. The discovery of tin in the 1880s brought more activity, but a real boom came in 1890 when the Burlington Railroad built to the town and the Harney Peak Tin Company placed its headquarters there. One observer counted fifteen saloons on Main Street, with another describing it as "a town with a church on each end and a mile of hell in between." The census reflects Hill City's booms and busts: the 1880 census showed no population, then in 1890 the census taker counted 479 people. A Black Hills newspaper from that time, however, estimated 1,200 residents, which may have been closer to the truth. But as the tin boom collapsed in the 1890s, the town had to rely on a few small hardrock gold mines, such as the J.R., the Golden Slipper, and the Sunbeam, and the intermittent output of a few pegmatite mines. The town's population dwindled from 602 people in 1900 to 213 in 1910 and neared zero in 1920. When a fire hit in 1902, newspapers reported that several of the destroyed buildings were empty.

**1880 Train:** Hill City saw a small recovery when Mount Rushmore and Custer State Park began attracting visitors in the 1930s. It got a bigger boost when Bill Heckman started the Black Hills Central Railroad (BHCRR), calling it the 1880 Train, in 1957. In an effort to emulate historic mountain railroading, Heckman laid a third rail between the existing standard gauge tracks to create a narrow gauge line for five miles from Hill City to Oblivion, a small stopover he built. Heckman used narrow gauge equipment until 1965, when he converted his operation to standard gauge and extended the tourist train to Keystone to attract more riders. While this brought extra business, Heckman seemed more interested in buying and selling equipment than in running a tourist attraction. The rail yard was littered with junk, and the tourist operation appeared shabby. At one time Heckman dreamed of creating an Old West town. After he acquired some western-looking structures, little happened. In 1990, Bob and Jo Anna Warder bought the property and turned it into a well-kept, well-run operation. They fixed up the equipment, cleaned the yards, and bought new motive power, including two large mallet steam locomotives. These engines attract rail fans from across the country. Today, the Warders' daughter, Meg, runs the tourist line.

**South Dakota State Railroad Museum:** The Warders are also responsible for the railroad museum. Not long after buying the 1880 Train, they officially organized a museum, but it was slow to develop. In 2004 they put artifacts in a Pullman rail car, and in 2010 they built the current museum structure. Since the 1880 Train is the most viable tourist rail line in the state, Hill City seemed to be a natural location for a railroad museum, and the Warders convinced the legislature to recognize it as the "state railroad" museum. Still, people in such places as Aberdeen, which has a significant rail history, wondered why they should not have the state railroad museum. Although the museum is financially independent of the railroad, it uses railroad property, and the operating agreement limits what it can display outside as well as what its gift shop can sell. Some of the nation's more successful railroad museums have rail yards filled with equipment and depend on large gift shop sales. These limitations have hurt the museum's flexibility. Nevertheless, rail expert Rick Mills is the director and curator, and he has worked diligently to create a first-rate museum.

**Hill City transformation:** Much as the 1880 Train has changed over the years, Hill City has also been transformed. In the 1960s, the town was a mixture of rundown buildings, dirty streets, and garish novelty shops. One attraction was the Hill City "artist," who painted in an open-air stand on Main Street, using four-inch paint brushes and black felt canvas. In the 1990s, more established or sophisticated artists opened studios, turning the town into an art center. Because he primarily paints Black Hills scenes, Jon Crane is probably the most famous. He opened a gallery in 1995 and moved to his current location in 1998. Besides becoming a vibrant art community, Hill City has attracted other upscale shops that have added to the town's transformation.

## Part Eight Sheridan Lake

Route Overview: From Mickelson Trailhead take Poplar Street to Hill City's Main Street. Follow Main Street, US 16, through town to its junction with US 385. Turn left (north) on US 385 to Sheridan Lake for a Recommended Stop.

Mileage starts at Tracy Park.

0.0 mi **Tracy Park, Hill City. Turn left onto Poplar Street.**

**At the junction of Poplar Street and US 16 Bypass, Railroad Avenue, go straight to cross the highway. After one block turn right (north) onto Hill City's Main Street.**

0.1 mi **Hill City Main Street, turn right.**

0.2 mi ***Harney Peak Mining News* Building (1885), 301 Main Street:** Using long hand-hewn logs, German immigrant Camillo Von Woehrmann constructed the building at the corner of Main and McGregor Streets for a saloon and sleeping quarters in about 1885. He converted it into a newspaper office in 1890 and published the *Harney Peak Mining News* until he returned to Germany in 1922. After his departure, the structure housed a variety of businesses, including a night club, a car garage, and a fly-fishing shop. During these years, it was expanded and remodeled, including the application of stucco to the walls. It survived Hill City fires in 1891 and 1902 and a building fire in 1975. The last blaze, however, revealed the log structure hidden underneath the stucco. The owners decided to restore the logs, and after some investigation determined that it is the oldest commercial hand-hewn log building in South Dakota. The building has recently housed a restaurant.

0.3 mi **C. E. McEachron General Merchandise Building (1902), 261 Main Street:** Charles E. McEachron came to the Black Hills from New York around 1879. He worked on the Rockerville Flume for a time, then opened a general merchandise store at this location as Hill City experienced a small boom in 1890. After a 1902 fire destroyed his wood building, he built this large, two-story brick structure. For years it stood out as Hill City's biggest commercial front. McEachron stayed in business until the late 1920s. The building has since housed a variety of businesses, including a music venue known as Lit'l Nashville and an art gallery. It is currently home to a Harley-Davidson store.

0.4 mi **The Alpine Inn, 133 Main Street:** The Alpine Inn is a Hill City landmark. The restaurant has become famous for its cuisine. The building is a tangible reminder of the Harney Peak Tin Company, which built it in the late 1880s and early 1890s. Harney Peak Tin is more thoroughly discussed at the Keystone stop.

0.5 mi **The Black Hills Institute of Geological Research, 117 Main Street:** In a remodeled gymnasium on the same block as the Alpine Inn is the Black Hills Institute. Two paleontologists, brothers Neal and Peter Larson, opened the institute in 1974. While they hired out for paleontological digs, they also explored on their own, hoping to make a big find. Most famously, while excavating near Faith, South

The Alpine Inn Restaurant in Hill City, 1991. *South Dakota State Historical Society*

LITTLE TIGER LN
LOIS LN
MARSHALL GULCH RD
PENALUA RD
DEEGAN DR
BRADLEY GULCH RD
CHINA GULCH RD
SE
ROBINS ROOST RD
MINOR LAKE CIR
MAJOR LAKE RD
FRONTAGE RD
DEERFIELD RD
MUSEUM DR
CHUTE ROOSTER DR
QUINN DR
TOP O'HILL AVE
SMOKEY DR
PONDEROSA AVE
PINE AVE
WALNUT AVE
PINE MTN AVE
MARYBETH CT
FOREST ST
OLD HILL CTY RD
Hill City
16B
Start:
Tracy Park
NEWTON AVE
BISHOP MOUNTAIN DR

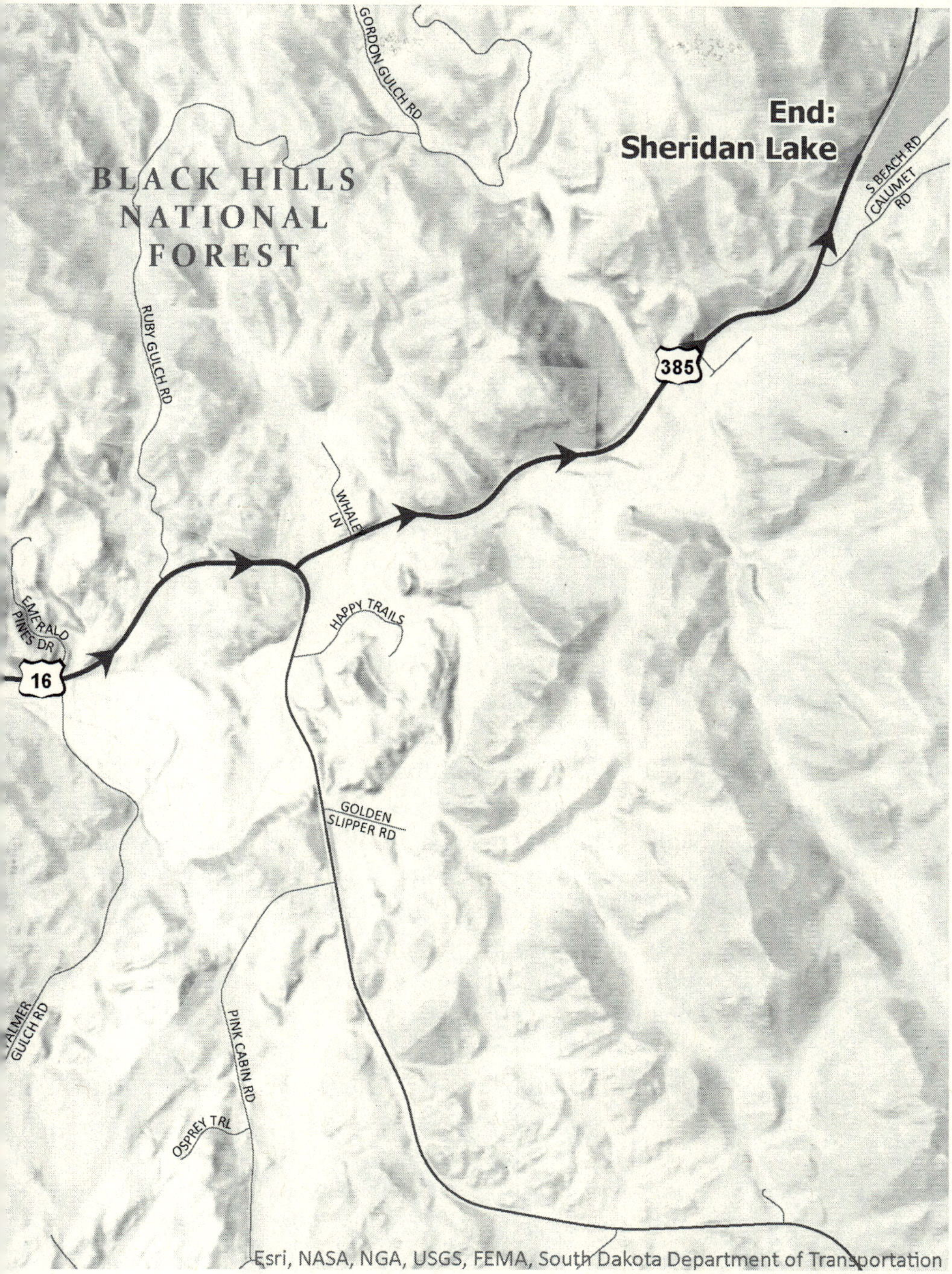
End:
Sheridan Lake
BLACK HILLS
NATIONAL
FOREST
GORDON GULCH RD
S BEACH RD
CALUMET
RD
385
RUBY GULCH RD
WHALE
LN
EMERALD
PINES DR
16
HAPPY TRAILS
GOLDEN
SLIPPER RD
PALMER
GULCH RD
PINK CABIN RD
OSPREY TRL
Esri, NASA, NGA, USGS, FEMA, South Dakota Department of Transportation

Dakota, on the Cheyenne River Indian Reservation in 1990, they uncovered Sue, the most complete Tyrannosaurus rex fossil ever found, and named it after the person who made the find, Sue Hendrickson. Peter Larson paid the property owner the $5,000 he requested and brought the fossil to Hill City. Many entities soon laid claim to the T. rex, however, including the property owner, the BIA, and the FBI. During the fight, the U.S. attorney for South Dakota had the National Guard haul Sue away in 1992. After a ten-year court battle, the property owner won claim to Sue and put it up for auction. Chicago's Field Museum bought the fossil for $8.4 million. In the process, Peter Larson was sent to jail for eighteen months on unrelated charges. CNN distributed a documentary called *Dinosaur 13* about Sue and the surrounding events.

**Stan:** The Larson brothers discovered another T. rex, Stan, just outside of Buffalo, South Dakota, in 1987 and unearthed it in 1992. Though not as complete as Sue, Stan is the second-most complete T. rex and has the most perfectly preserved skull ever found. That made the discovery valuable, and Stan became the centerpiece of the Black Hills Institute's collection. Several museums and collectors wanted to view Stan's skull, so the institute started selling castings for $100,000 each. It also rented castings for $20,000 a month. Stan has become the most duplicated dinosaur fossil in existence. The institute used the revenue to fund more fossil hunts and for other expenses. Sadly, a dispute between the brothers resulted in lawsuits. In the end, a judge ordered the institute's assets divided equally. Peter got the institute and the rights to Stan's castings, while Neal got Stan. The judge estimated the institute's worth at $5 million; Stan was estimated to be worth $6–8 million. Neal sold Stan to an anonymous bidder at an October 2020 auction for $31.8 million, the highest price ever paid for a fossil. As Peter said, "That's more than we've grossed in the entire history of our business." Peter has since restructured the institute.

0.9 mi **Chute Rooster:** A little south of the highway is the Chute Rooster restaurant. The structure was reportedly built in 1896 to lodge personnel of the Harney Peak Tin Mining Company. After the mining company closed, it was converted into a barn and later into a restaurant and bar.

**Frink Store:** Next to the Chute Rooster is a small building with a covered boardwalk and a false front, giving it the distinctive look of a small store. William Frink Jr. built the structure to house his general merchandise store at Mystic, fourteen miles up the road, around 1930. The building was moved to Hill City in the early 1970s.

1.2 mi **CCC Museum:** On the left-hand (north) side of the road is the Hill City Visitor Center. The Forest Service formerly used this structure for its Mystic Ranger District office. When the Forest Service relocated the Mystic office to Rapid City in 2006, Hill City acquired the building for a visitor center, which also houses a Civilian Conservation Corps museum. A statue titled *Work Call* stands in front. CCC veteran Melvin B. ("Sarge") Hermanson commissioned it in 2008 to honor the young men who worked in the CCC.

2.3 mi **Mitchell Lake:** On the right (southwest) side of the road is a small lake created when the CCC dammed Spring Creek. It is one of many

The Civilian Conservation Corps Museum of South Dakota, 2022. *Author photo*

small dams the CCC built, but this one has the distinction of being the first to use bentonite to seal cracks and faults in the bedrock that would have otherwise prevented the dam from holding water. The same technique was soon applied across the nation.

**Beetle kill:** Beetle-killed trees are evident in this area and in other locations of the Black Hills, such as around Rochford. When pine bark beetles attack a tree, its needles turn brown before it dies. Since the needles have fallen off the beetle-killed trees, the extent of loss is not as evident as when the bugs are active. The Forest Service website states that pine bark beetle populations are generally at endemic levels; this means that the bugs are always present, but only affect stressed or weakened trees, such as those struck by lightning. For reasons not fully understood, beetle populations periodically increase dramatically to epidemic levels. The first, and largest, recorded epidemic occurred from the late 1890s into the early 1900s, killing large sections of the forest. Several epidemics have happened since then, each lasting from eight to twenty years. The most recent epidemic began in 1996 and ended in 2016. Thinning and controlled burns are often used to limit the possibility of an epidemic.

3.3 mi **Rushmore Forest Products:** The sawmill that sat at this location opened as the Stauter mill in 1968. It was sold five years later to the Edward Hines Company, a large operation that also owned sawmills in Colorado and Wyoming. Hines expanded the Hill City mill to the point that it became the largest private employer in the central Black Hills, with over 150 people either cutting trees or milling lumber. Because of a depressed market, Hines sold to the Continental Lumber Company in 1983. Neiman Enterprises, a family-owned business out of Hulett, Wyoming, bought the complex in 1998 and renamed it Rushmore Forest Products. The Neimans maintain that the Forest Service forced them to close it in 2021 by reducing the number of trees that could be harvested. The federal agency argues that previous logging activities and beetle kills have severely limited the number of marketable trees in the Black Hills, necessitating the cutback. Reduced harvests have caused quite a stir in the timber industry in recent years. Other mills very well may close.

3.6 mi **Prairie Berry:** This family-run winery produced its first commercial wine in Mobridge, South Dakota, in 1999. The owners moved south of Rapid City two years later, and then built their Hill City facility in 2004. With a robust business that continued to expand, they opened the Miner Brewing Co. in 2013 and an events center, which was the white structure on the far right, in 2014. The events center building once housed the Mistletoe Ranch, a store that sold Christmas merchandise year-round. The building originally stood in the town of Pactola on Rapid Creek and was relocated to this area when Pactola Dam was constructed in the 1950s. After twenty-five years of business, it was announced that Prairie Berry Winery would close at the end of 2024.

4.0 mi **Junction of US 16 & US 385, Three Forks. Take US 385 to the left (north).** This tour has paralleled Spring Creek since leaving Hill City and will continue to do so while following US 385 to Sheridan Lake. Prospectors made the Black Hills' second gold discovery along this creek, near Hill City. After that find, gold seekers came through this area as they looked for more of the yellow metal in Spring Creek.

6.0 mi **Recommended Stop at the Sheridan Lake pull-off:** An interpretative sign at the pull-off helps explain the area's history. Sheridan Lake is fed by Spring Creek, one of the four creeks in the southern and central Black Hills that carried gold (the other three were French, Castle, and Rapid Creeks). This diminutive creek flows through Hill City, fills Mitchell and Sheridan Lakes, passes Reptile Gardens, and then exits the Black Hills north of Hart Ranch, eventually draining into the Cheyenne River.

**Golden City:** Prospectors discovered gold along Spring Creek in the summer of 1875, but General Crook quickly removed most of these trespassers. In early 1876, soon after the army quit guarding the Black Hills, the gold diggers returned and established Golden City. With the usual mix of saloons, gambling halls, and general stores, Golden City was the third camp founded in the Black Hills, following Hill City and Custer City. Despite the name, the gold proved spotty. Some claims yielded good amounts of gold, while others produced nothing. A group from Montana reportedly took out $1,600 in March 1876, and another claim owner found enough gold to attract claim jumpers. He had to hold them off with a shotgun, and his location became known as Stand-off Bar. As with Custer City and Hill City, before long most of the prospectors left for Deadwood Gulch, though some stayed behind.

**Sheridan:** As people trickled back hoping to find undiscovered wealth in 1877, Golden City gained new life and the residents changed its name to Sheridan, after Civil War hero General Philip H. Sheridan. Now in command of the Military Division of the Missouri, he had purview over the Black Hills. Naming the town after the general may have been a way to honor him, but it was more likely a ploy to win political support. A group of Dakota Territory politicians had acquired land around Sheridan and formed the Black Hills Town Company with the goal of selling it at a profit. Dakota Territory governor John L. Pennington and congressional delegate Jefferson Parish Kidder were apparently involved, and they persuaded President Rutherford B. Hayes to place the U.S. Land Office in the town in March 1877. In April, when the legislature created Pennington County, Sheridan became the county seat. The Yankton and Deadwood papers damned these actions as political tricks, with one article stating that the operatives were part of a political ring. The plan soon collapsed anyway. Complaints from Deadwood convinced the commissioner of the U.S. Land Office to move the Black Hills office there in late 1877, and Pennington County voters chose Rapid City as the new county seat in November.

In October 1877, prior to losing its prominence, Sheridan had the honor of hosting the first term of the district court in the Black Hills, with federal judge Granville Bennett presiding. Because of the number of cases affecting Deadwood, many people made the trip, including those who just wanted "to see the fun." The visitors even imported an entire saloon. Sheridan was overwhelmed, forcing people to sleep wherever they could, including on the floor of the log cabin courthouse. Nevertheless, Bennett held court without a problem, and the log cabin became known as the Black Hills' "first courthouse." A crude sign stating that fact was later placed in front of the building. A fire destroyed the cabin in 1895.

A wagon road and a few nearby gold mines provided some business for the struggling camp. Local optimists also dreamed of developing area copper deposits. The 1875 Newton–Jenney Expedition had identified copper outcroppings in the mountain that sits just east of today's Sheridan Lake, earning it the name Blue Lead Mountain. Over the years, several people tried to recover the copper, which included building a small smelter. The most famous operation was the Dakota–Calumet. In the end, little copper was produced, but the miners left numerous small tunnels and a shaft. With copper mines in Michigan and Montana dominating the market, any copper operation would have struggled to compete.

**Rockerville:** This gold camp sat several miles east of Sheridan, but residents still watched its development with interest. Gold was discovered along a branch of Spring Creek in 1876, but a lack of water made it difficult to recover. The camp eventually became known as Rockerville, named after a piece of mining equipment that could recover gold with little water: the "rocker" or "rocker box." The claim owners, however, wanted better results and decided to build a flume to transport water from Spring Creek, near Sheridan, to Rockerville. It took from 1878 to 1880 to build the seventeen-mile flume, and although it leaked, it worked well enough to allow for hydraulic mining, in which water pressure is used to wash away overburden and expose the gold. About $500,000 of gold was recovered before it closed. The flume's legacy lives on; its path has been turned into one of the Black Hills' most popular hiking trails. The trail may be accessed on the east side of Sheridan Lake.

**Logging:** Timber harvesting came to the Sheridan area in 1908 when the Lanphere-Hinrichs Lumber Company built a railroad into the Victoria Creek drainage, about five miles northeast of Sheridan, and began harvesting trees for its Rapid City sawmill. The Warren-Lamb Company bought Lanphere-Hinrichs in 1914 and moved the timber operations to Custer State Park. They returned to the Sheridan area in 1926 and built a railroad spur into the Spring Creek drainage and

People fishing at Sheridan Lake, undated.
*South Dakota State Historical Society*

eventually through where Sheridan Lake is today. Warren-Lamb abandoned rail operations and turned to trucks when the CCC began constructing the dam in 1938. The company continued logging until its sawmill burned in 1954. Evidence of the railroad's bed remains along Spring Creek.

**Sheridan Lake:** Sheridan Lake, like most Black Hills lakes, was a New Deal project. In 1937, a variety of agencies, including the Forest Service, the South Dakota Game Commission, the Izaak Walton League (an environmental organization founded in 1922 to promote natural resource protection and outdoor recreation), and federal relief programs, developed a plan to dam Spring Creek and create a 400-acre lake. To generate interest in the project, officials held a naming contest. The winner was "Lake o' the Pines," but most people continued calling it Sheridan Lake, and the new name was soon dropped. CCC workers, under Forest Service supervision, finished the dam in 1941, creating the largest CCC-built lake in the Black Hills. Sadly, twenty feet of water covered the former gold camp. The U.S. Forest Service still owns the lake, and unlike dams controlled by the U.S. Army Corps of Engineers and the Bureau of Reclamation, there is no domestic or industrial call on the water. Instead, it is dedicated to recreation and to maintaining Spring Creek's fishery, so the water level remains stable throughout the year.

## Part Nine Pactola

Route Overview: From Sheridan Lake, travel north on US 385 to Pactola Lake for a Recommended Stop.

Mileage starts at Sheridan Lake.

0.0 mi **Sheridan Lake, Rapid City. Return to US 385 and travel north.**

2.3 mi **Camp 15:** This road's name is a reminder of the area's logging past. The Warren-Lamb Lumber Company established many remote logging camps to supply its Rapid City sawmill in the early twentieth century. Like most logging companies, instead of applying names to these temporary locations, Warren-Lamb just numbered them sequentially. "Camp 15" was up this road. A few other Black Hills roads carry similar names and often refer to former logging sites.

5.5 mi **Black Forest Inn:** The road to the west, Forest Service Road 258, goes to a bed & breakfast known as the Black Forest Inn. Bernice Musekamp built the large log structure in 1953–1954 to replace a lodge and restaurant that she had operated at the townsite of Pactola since 1937. The construction of Pactola Dam forced her to relocate. She used the same name at both locations: Moosecamp Lodge (also spelled Moose Camp or Musekamp). Carl and Kay Burgess renamed it the Black Forest Inn after purchasing the lodge from Musekamp in 1962. The building has since been sold and remodeled.

7.7 mi **Bullock Lookout:** In the far distance to the west is a fire tower named after Seth Bullock, a pioneer sheriff and early Black Hills Forest supervisor. The lookout sits on 5,922-foot Scruton Mountain, named for two brothers who owned a nearby mine. The CCC built a wooden lookout tower there in 1939. It was replaced with a fifty-three-foot steel tower and demolished in 1975. The lookout is staffed only during periods of high fire danger.

Silver City
Johnson Siding
End:
Pactola Lake
BLACK HILLS
NATIONAL
FOREST
385
44
Start:
Sheridan Lake
PACTOLA BASIN RD
BEAR GULCH RD
EDELWEISS MOUNTAIN RD
PACTOLA RD
CUSTER GULCH RD
BRUSH CREEK RD
PACTOLA DR
S SPRING CREEK RD
CLEAR CREEK LN
VICTORIA LAKE RD
TRACK RD
TAYLOR RANCH RD
HORSE CREEK RD
S VICTORIA RD
LOG CABIN RD
HEALD TRL
SHERIDAN LAKE RD
NORTHBEACH RD
DAKOTA POINT RD
BAKER PARK RD
GORDON GULCH RD
LOGCABIN RD
RUBY GULCH RD
BEACH RD
CALUMET RD
JOHNSON GULCH RD
PENALUA RD
CHINA GULCH RD
Esri, NASA, NGA, USGS, FEMA, South Dakota Department of Transportatio

The old wooden Seth Bullock Lookout Tower on Scruton Mountain, as viewed from the new steel tower, 1966. *Black Hills National Forest Historical Collection*

8.4 mi **Recommended Stop at Pactola Dam.**

**Rapid Creek:** Pactola Dam is fed by Rapid Creek, which includes water from North Rapid, Rapid, Slate, and Castle Creeks. Rapid Creek's headwaters begin near the Wyoming state line, flowing through the Black Hills and onto the plains where it meets the Cheyenne River about six miles east of Rapid City. It is one of the Black Hills' main drainages, along with Spearfish and Whitewood Creeks.

**Humans along Rapid Creek:** Rapid Creek has a long history of human occupation. Native peoples followed its course in and out of the Black Hills, as whites did later. For instance, John Brennan and a few other prospectors left their placer workings in Palmer Gulch and followed Rapid Creek out of the Black Hills. They established

Rapid City along its course in February 1876. Settlements and activities along Rapid Creek have included mining camps, timber camps, health resorts, and vacation retreats.

**Gold:** Prospectors searched for gold along Rapid Creek in 1875, with at least ten men staking claims by 1876. While they found some gold, it was not in paying quantities (the amount needed to return more than a day's wages). Nevertheless, towns took root. Camp Crook, named in honor of the general, formed in the broad valley where Pactola Lake is today. Once the U.S. government annexed the Black Hills from the Great Sioux Reservation, the number of residents surged to 300. Despite the limited quantities of gold, the camp gained a hotel and a general store. A Deadwood-to-Custer wagon road also passed through the valley, providing trade for the businesses. The town faltered as most people moved on to Deadwood Gulch in 1876. When that excitement died down, the little camp came back to life, but the residents decided to change its name. Travelers had consistently confused it with Crook City, a town east of Deadwood. One man suggested Pactola, a reference to Pactolus, the Lydian river of golden sands, now known as Sart Çayı, on the Aegean coast of Turkey. According to myth, the legendary King Midas enriched the Pactolus with gold while bathing in its waters. Despite the optimistic name, only limited quantities of gold were found near Pactola or along Rapid Creek.

**Rapid Canyon Railroad:** Miners and merchants managed to keep Pactola alive over the years. A small boom came when the Rapid Canyon Line Railroad (RCL) built through in 1906. This little rail line has a long and convoluted history. It went by many names, but the RCL is probably the most descriptive. It began in 1886 when attorney William T. Coad conceived of building a railroad to the mines in the central Black Hills and turning Rapid City into a mining center. It took time for his idea to develop, but by 1891 he had decided to build his rail line from Rapid City to Mystic, up Rapid Canyon. Not only would this route reach the mines, but it would also connect with the newly constructed Burlington Railroad at Mystic. With the railroads exchanging freight and passengers, Coad forecast reduced transportation costs for Rapid City. As he raised money and started building his

The Rapid Canyon Line, undated. *South Dakota State Historical Society*

little line, he found the project much more expensive and difficult to complete than he envisioned. After thirteen years of struggle, he had only managed to build a few miles of track. He went broke in 1904, and the line sold at foreclosure. His primary contractor, C. D. Crouch, purchased it. Crouch managed to raise the money to finish the thirty-two-mile railroad, which included constructing over 100 bridges. What was now called the Crouch Line opened on 26 March 1906.

The Crouch Line seemed doomed from the start. A year after it opened, a flood washed out many of its bridges. After rebuilding, the company suffered several accidents, some of which resulted in fatalities and expensive litigation. Then the railroad failed to draw enough traffic to profit. It survived by hauling logs for the Warren-Lamb Lumber Company and by transporting tourists, sightseers, fisher-people, and campers. As it struggled to make money, the owners threatened to abandon the line, but Rapid City businessmen, led by C. C. Warren and C. T. Lamb, saved it in 1920. World War II brought a small surge in traffic. The railroad carried troops out of Rapid City and hauled tank cars of fuel into town for the new Rapid City Army Air Base (now Ellsworth AFB). But the lack of wartime labor caused maintenance to be deferred, and the line deteriorated, leading to its abandonment in 1947.

**Bernice Musekamp:** The town's most famous resident was Bernice Musekamp. She opened a small store in Pactola to serve auto and rail travelers in 1926, but she altered her business over the years. In the 1930s, she added a dance hall and restaurant, and at one point she opened what was called Moosecamp Lodge or Moosecamp Park. It consisted of a restaurant, eleven cabins, an icehouse, and a hunting lodge.

**Prohibition:** The outlawing of alcohol in the 1920s brought moonshiners to the area. The remote location offered some advantages: the railroad brought in corn and other grains, the creek provided water, and the Black Hills offered plenty of hiding places. The proliferation of stills led to the area's nickname, "the valley of a thousand smokes." The illicit liquor reportedly brought interesting people to town, including Poker Alice Tubbs, who purchased supplies for her brothel in Sturgis.

**Depression Era Gold Rush:** Another minor boom developed when the federal government raised the price of gold during the Depression. Gold seekers prospected all along Rapid Creek. Some of their holes and waste piles are still evident, especially west of Pactola Lake.

**The end of Pactola:** When the Bureau of Reclamation started developing Pactola Dam in 1946, it brought an end to the little settlement. Musekamp and other landholders were forced to sell to the Bureau. Some of the buildings were relocated, the rest demolished. One structure went to the Hill City area and was eventually incorporated into the Prairie Berry Winery complex.

**Damming Rapid Creek:** Developers had envisioned building dams in the Rapid Creek drainage since settlers first arrived. The first significant effort came in 1890 when the Upper Rapid City Company built Canyon Lake Dam as part of a planned resort four miles above Rapid City.

During the Depression and drought of the 1930s, the Bureau of Reclamation built dams and irrigation districts across the West. Surveyors from the Bureau examined Rapid Creek's drainage in 1937 and developed the Rapid Valley Project. It included money to build dams at Pactola and Deerfield (on Castle Creek), and to create an irrigation district of 12,000 acres in Rapid Valley. The Pactola portion, however, stalled because the irrigation users would have had to pay for relocating the railroad and highway that ran through the valley, making the project too expensive. Despite the setback, the government moved ahead with Deerfield Dam, completing it in 1946.

**Pactola Dam:** The Pactola project came back to life when the Missouri River flooded in the 1940s. This got the U.S. Army Corps of Engineers involved, the agency in charge of controlling flood waters and navigation. Both the Corps and the Bureau of Reclamation investigated the Missouri River drainage, looking for possible dam locations, but with different intentions. The Corps had flood control in mind, while the Bureau worried about irrigation. Each developed their own plan. Congress asked for a compromise, resulting in the Pick-Sloan Plan (Pick was with the Corps and Sloan with the Bureau). The resulting authorization became known as the Missouri River Basin Project of 1944. It called for the construction of six dams on the Missouri River, with four in South Dakota, to be managed by the Corps. Additional dams on the river's tributaries would be managed by the Bureau. After investigating Black Hills locations, the Bureau authorized Angostura Dam on the Cheyenne River in the southern Black Hills, and it reauthorized the Pactola project. When the railroad through Rapid Canyon closed in 1947, one major obstacle had been removed. Construction on Pactola Dam began in 1952 and was completed in 1956. The reservoir was designed to hold 99,000 acre feet of water (an acre foot is approximately 326,000 gallons), of which 43,000 acre feet were left empty for flood control storage. Conservation storage amounted to 55,000 acre feet and dead storage totaled 1,000 acre feet.

**Rapid City Flood of 1972:** The most significant flood to hit the Rapid Creek drainage was the Black Hills flood of 1972. A government study estimated that Pactola prevented $434,000 of losses in Rapid City—unfortunately, the city suffered over $100 million in damages. The heaviest rainfall was on the Black Hills' eastern slope, below the dam.

**Dam modifications:** A 1982 safety evaluation found that a "once in a century" flood would top the existing dam by six feet for approximately eight hours, causing it to fail and putting Rapid City underwater. The Bureau of Reclamation raised the dam fifteen feet and widened the spillway. Some skeptics have argued that the Bureau undertook the project to keep the agency busy after the federal government had ended the era of building big western dams.

**Water allocation:** The Bureau of Reclamation developed Pactola Dam and the Rapid Valley Project primarily for irrigation. Under a 1952 contract, irrigators controlled more than 60 percent of Pactola's water, or just over 34,000 acre feet per year. Ellsworth AFB and Rapid City were allocated about 26 percent, or 14,500 acre feet. The Bureau of Reclamation kept 6,000 acre feet for fish and wildlife conservation. When the original contract expired in 1992, the various entities began talks to reallocate the water. It took thirteen years, but in 2005, the city, the Rapid Valley Conservation District, and the Bureau of Reclamation finally agreed to turn over 89 percent of the lake's water, or 49,000 acre feet, to Rapid City. The Bureau retained the remainder. The irrigators agreed to the change with the understanding that they still had access to 8,000 acre feet in Deerfield Dam, and that they no longer had to cover the majority of Pactola's operating expenses. Although the city took over the costs, the Rapid City negotiators saw the agreement as the best way to guarantee a long-term water source. Ironically, the city gets most of its water from wells drilled into the Madison Aquifer because well water requires less treatment and costs less to supply than lake water.

**Silver City:** Located at the western tip of Pactola Lake, Silver City started out as Camp Gorman, named after the Gorman brothers. The three brothers reportedly developed two mines and uncovered some valuable ore in the area, but one died and the other two left before doing much with it. As reports of mineral-bearing rock spread, more people arrived and the camp became known as Silver City. It grew to about 300 people by 1878. Outside of a few mines in Sunnyside Gulch, north of town, the area yielded little wealth. Some residents blamed confusion over the type of metal, with reports mentioning everything from gold to antimony. Others claimed that the ore needed to be treated in a smelter. A bright future seemed assured when a smelter opened in Rapid City and the Rapid Canyon Line built through in the early twentieth century, but little ore was ever mined. Instead, the railroad primarily hauled logs to Warren-Lamb's sawmill in Rapid City. Today Silver City is home to a handful of full-time and part-time residents.

**Silver City mineral exploration:** The possibility of renewed mining just north of Silver City has become a concern in recent years. Since 2018, a Minneapolis exploration company known as F3 Gold has sought permission to drill forty-two test holes on federal and private land. Based on an updated geologic model, the company believes that an undiscovered gold deposit exists in the area. Under federal law, it has the right to drill on National Forest land, so long as it follows federal guidelines. The company has worked hard to win over nearby residents but has still met considerable resistance. Rapid City's Council voted against the project in early 2020. While F3 Gold continues to seek permission to drill, the Forest Service has been debating whether to withdraw the area from mineral location.

## Part Ten

# Rimrock Highway to Rapid City

Route Overview: From Pactola Lake, travel north on US 385 to junction with SD 44. Turn right (east). Travel toward Rapid City, watching for signs pointing to locations that correspond with the narrative. Once in Rapid City, follow SD 44, Jackson Boulevard, to its junction with Sheridan Lake Road. Take a left on Sheridan Lake Road and follow that road to West Main Street. Turn right (east) on West Main Street and follow it into downtown Rapid City.

Mileage starts at Pactola Lake.

0.0 mi **Pactola Lake, Rapid City. Return to US 385 and travel north.**

2.1 mi **Junction with SD 44:** Rimrock Highway, or SD 44, roughly parallels Rapid Creek as it flows to Rapid City. The road provides access to many of the historic locations in Rapid Canyon. The word "rimrock" refers to the cliffs that tower over the creek in several places.

4.5 mi **Placerville:** Placerville is about one mile below Pactola Dam along the creek. Today it is the location of a United Church of Christ camp, but as the name implies, it once supported placer mining. The first major mining operation came when New York developer L. A. Richards founded the Bed Rock Gold Mining Company in 1902. He claimed to have a low-cost, high-volume placer machine that could profitably recover gold from Rapid Creek. Over the next eight years, Richards and another operator constructed a small dam at Pactola, built trestles and ditches for a three-mile flume, and installed hydraulic nozzles and sluicing equipment. The operation, however, failed to pay. Despite its poor showing, prospectors continued to explore the area, especially during the Depression, but Placerville never again received much attention.

**Electrical generation:** While Richards struggled with his gold operation, he became convinced that the volume and velocity of water in Rapid Creek could be used to generate electricity. By 1907, he started extending his flume to a location below Placerville where he envisioned building a hydroelectric plant, but his efforts came to naught. He ended up selling his water rights, ditch, and flume to Rapid City businessman George Mansfield, founder of the Dakota Power Company, which would eventually extend the flume farther down Rapid Creek to Big Bend.

**Placerville Retreat:** After the placer operations closed, Placerville's attractive setting and convenient location on the Rapid Canyon Line attracted picnickers and campers. The Congregational church has hosted summer camps there since 1920.

**Johnson Siding:** About a mile below Placerville is Johnson Siding. In 1892, a family of Swedish immigrants homesteaded on land around Rapid Creek and opened a sawmill, cutting timber from their own land and from neighboring parcels. It was generally a small operation, supplying local needs, but they sometimes handled large orders. During the construction of the railroad down Rapid Canyon, the Johnsons supplied ties and bridge timbers. Once the line opened in 1906, the railroad established a rail stop and siding near the sawmill, naming it "Johnson Siding." With better transportation, the Johnsons saw their market double. Another boost in business came when the Dakota Power Company used Johnson lumber to extend L. A. Richards's flume to Big Bend, completing it in 1912. The Johnson family occasionally moved their sawmill to be closer to uncut timber, but they have been out of business for some time.

8.2–8.4 mi **Cliff above Rapid Creek:** The high cliff wall is part of the rimrock that runs along Rapid Creek. In this area, evidence of the water flume that brought water from near Pactola to the Big Bend power plant can be seen when the light is right.

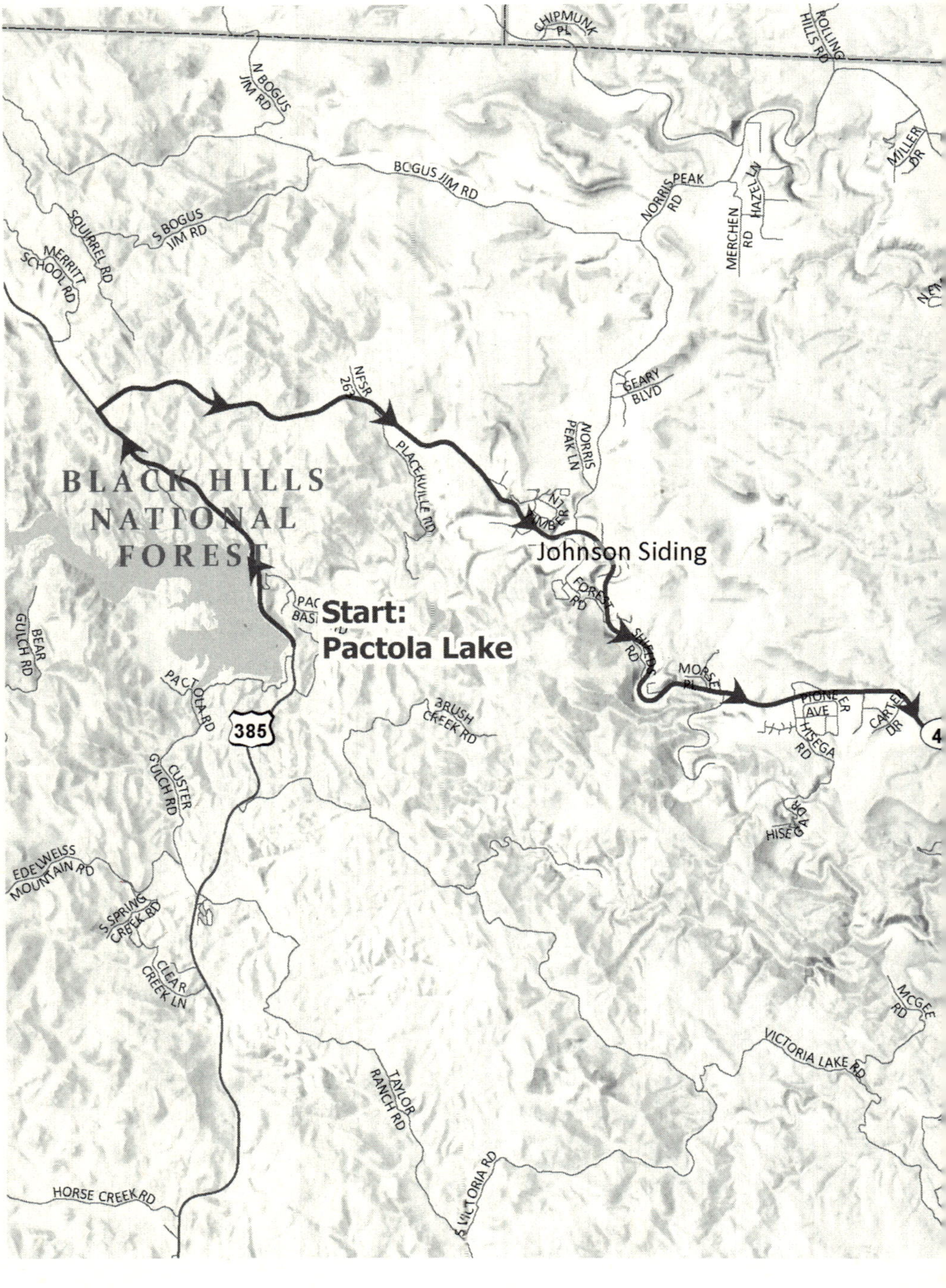
CHIPMUNK PL
ROLLING HILLS RD
N BOGUS JIM RD
MILLER DR
BOGUS JIM RD
NORRIS PEAK RD
HAZEL LN
MERCHEN RD
S BOGUS JIM RD
SQUIRREL RD
MERRITT SCHOOL RD
NFSR 263
GEARY BLVD
NORRIS PEAK LN
PLACERVILLE RD
BLACK HILLS NATIONAL FOREST
Johnson Siding
FOREST RD
Start: Pactola Lake
BEAR GULCH RD
MORSE PL
PIONEER AVE
CARTER DR
PACTOLA RD
385
BRUSH CREEK RD
HISEGA RD
CUSTER GULCH RD
HISEGA DR
EDELWEISS MOUNTAIN RD
S SPRING CREEK RD
CLEAR CREEK LN
MCGEE RD
VICTORIA LAKE RD
TAYLOR RANCH RD
S VICTORIA RD
HORSE CREEK RD

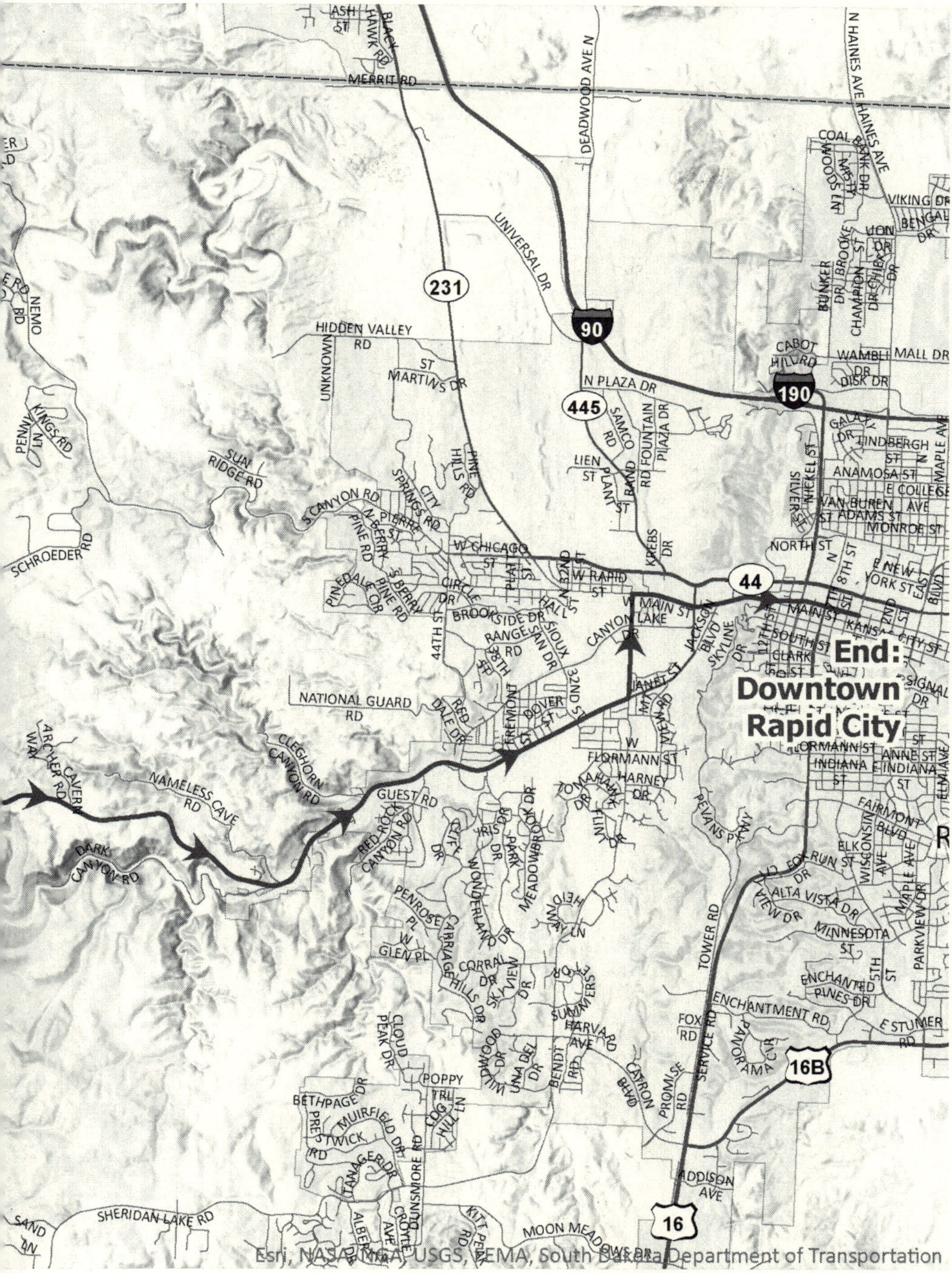
End:
Downtown
Rapid City
231
90
190
445
44
16B
16
MERRIT RD
BLACK HAWK RD
DEADWOOD AVE N
N HAINES AVE
HAINES AVE
COAL BANK DR
UNIVERSAL DR
HIDDEN VALLEY RD
UNKNOWN
ST MARTIN'S DR
N PLAZA DR
SAMCO RD
FOUNTAIN PLAZA DR
LIEN ST
PLANT ST
RAND RD
KREBS DR
PINE HILLS RD
CITY SPRINGS RD
S CANYON RD
SUN RIDGE RD
SCHROEDER RD
NEMO RD
KINGS RD
W CHICAGO ST
W RAPID ST
W MAIN ST
CANYON LAKE DR
JACKSON BLVD
SKYLINE DR
MAIN ST
KANSAS CITY ST
SOUTH ST
CLARK ST
NORTH ST
N MAPLE AVE
E NEW YORK ST
NATIONAL GUARD RD
CLEGHORN CANYON RD
NAMELESS CAVE RD
ARCHER RD
CAVERN WAY
DARK CANYON RD
GUEST RD
RED ROCK CANYON RD
BROOKSIDE DR
FREMONT ST
DOVER ST
32ND ST
W FLORMANN ST
HARNEY DR
TOMAHAWK DR
FLORMANN ST
INDIANA ST
E INDIANA ST
FAIRMONT BLVD
ELK ST
FOX RUN ST
ALTA VISTA DR
MINNESOTA ST
TOWER RD
ENCHANTED PINES DR
ENCHANTMENT RD
E STUMER RD
PANORAMA CIR
SERVICE RD
CATRON BLVD
PROMISE RD
ADDISON AVE
SHERIDAN LAKE RD
MOON MEADOWS DR
KITT PEAK RD
DUNSMORE RD
CLOUD PEAK DR
POPPY TRL
BETHPAGE DR
MUIRFIELD DR
PRESTWICK RD
TANAGER DR
SAND LN
WONDERLAND DR
MEADOWBROOK DR
CORRAL DR
SKY VIEW DR
CARRIAGE HILLS DR
PENROSE PL
GLEN PL
WILDWOOD DR
UNA DEL DR
BENDT RD
HARVARD AVE
SUMMERSET DR
Esri, NASA, NGA, USGS, FEMA, South Dakota Department of Transportation

9.1 mi **Big Bend:** About two miles below Johnson Siding is Big Bend, named after a bend in Rapid Creek. Here Dakota Power opened its hydroelectric plant in 1912, but an inconsistent water supply interfered with operations. The water froze in the winter and disappeared during dry periods. Financial problems also dogged the company. Nevertheless, the plant operated until the company sold the equipment during World War II. Today the old hydro plant is a bed & breakfast.

**Thunderhead Falls and Fort Meade Hydraulic Company:** A tourist attraction called Thunderhead Falls once stood three and a half miles below Pactola Dam, around the corner from the power plant. It featured a 600-foot-long tunnel with a waterfall at the end. Today the attraction is closed, but water still flows through the tunnel. The Fort Meade Hydraulic Gold Mining Company, with Robert Flormann in charge, started the tunnel in the fall of 1879. The company's name reportedly came from officers at Fort Meade who had invested, but Flormann may have used it to give his operation creditability. In any case, Flormann's idea was to drain the creek at Big Bend by diverting the water through the tunnel, dig into the exposed creek bed, and uncover a fortune in gold-ladened gravel. He would then use the water rushing through his tunnel to recover the gold in a sluice box. The company closed by 1882 before the tunnel was finished. A local newspaper later scolded Flormann for squandering money on useless work. Without saying so, the paper, and many others, suspected Flormann of doing just enough work to keep his investors happy while he pocketed most of the money.

**Big Bend Hydraulic Company:** In 1883, a year after Fort Meade Hydraulic closed, the Big Bend Hydraulic Company was formed and followed a similar pattern. It promised to finish the tunnel, expose the creek, and sluice the gold out of the gravel. Over the next four years, the operatives declared at least thirty-eight dividends, paying out nearly $150,000 to investors, but the money did not come from gold production—it came from selling more and more stock, which was easy to do since the company was declaring dividends. Local people denounced it as a fraud, and T. H. White, a local mining engineer, decried the situation in an article in the *Engineering and Mining Jour-*

The Pierre Lodge at Hisega, 2022. Local artists have made the lodge famous by featuring it in their paintings. *Author photo*

*nal*. Although the company sued White for libel, it was indeed a fraud, and the operators disappeared by 1889.

The upshot of these two operations was a 600-foot tunnel, which got close enough to the creek on the other side of the hill to punch a hole in the creek bed. Water flowed through the hole, creating a waterfall and a small stream in the tunnel. Other gold companies later worked this area but failed to find much gold.

9.7 mi **Hisega and Pierre Lodge:** Pierre Lodge sits about 1.3 miles down Hisega Road. After the Rapid Canyon Line opened the beauty of the canyon in 1906, summer fun enthusiasts flocked to the creek. In due time, many recreational sites popped up. The railroad even joined in the fun, establishing a fishing resort, Red Dog at the Needles, near the junction of Slate and Rapid Creeks in 1909.

A year earlier, a group of picnickers had such a delightful time at the future site of Pierre Lodge that they gave it a name. Combining the first initials of the six young ladies at the picnic, they came up with "Hisega." The next year, South Dakota businessmen created the

Pierre Lodge Association and built the existing lodge. Local artists, such as Dick DuBois, have found the structure to be a compelling subject, and their paintings have made it famous.

11.9 mi **Falling Rock Road:** This road provides access to an overlook on the edge of Rapid Canyon known as Falling Rock. It provides a good view of the canyon, the creek, and the railroad bed. Because of the high canyon walls, this area is popular with rock climbers and hikers. Unfortunately, several fatal accidents have resulted. If you wish to visit the Falling Rock overlook, there are two parking areas: one is near the intersection of Falling Rock Road and SD 44, and the other is 0.7 miles down Falling Rock Road. In either case, there is a footpath to the rim of Rapid Canyon.

12.6 mi **Black Hills Caverns:** Cavern Road leads to a former tourist cave known as Black Hills Caverns. Stories vary about how it was discovered. One states that prospectors found the cave in 1882, while another says that George Bennett discovered it in 1911 or 1915. Regardless of who discovered it, Bennett sold "Bennett's Wind Cave" to Rapid City physician William Morse in 1939. Morse had geology students from the School of Mines explore it, and he widened the passages to make it more accessible. Spotting bobcats and mountain lions in the area, he renamed it Wildcat Cave. Morse offered cave tours for nearly three decades, finally selling the attraction in the 1970s. The new owners renamed it Black Hills National Cave and then Black Hills Caverns.

14.5 mi **Dark Canyon Road:** Rimrock Highway meets Rapid Creek and Dark Canyon Road as it nears Rapid City. For a short distance, Dark Canyon Road sits on the roadbed of the former RCL railroad, providing access to several homes. Locals disagree on whether Rapid Canyon or a narrow side canyon is the true "Dark Canyon."

14.6 mi **Nameless Cave:** Located at the end of Nameless Cave Road, Nameless Cave was discovered sometime in the early twentieth century, after several other Black Hills caves had already become tourist attractions. The owners decided to follow suit in 1929 because of the cave's proximity to Rapid City and its abundance of calcite crystals. Why they chose to call it Nameless Cave is unclear. One explanation is that they never selected a name. Another claims that the skeleton of an unknown person was found in the cave. At one point, the owners had a contest to pick a new name, but the voters favored Nameless Cave. New owners renamed it Diamond Crystal Cave. Though "Diamond" was later dropped from the name, billboards featuring a diamond became common sights around the Black Hills. The 1972 flood inundated the cave, covering the crystals with mud. It went through a series of ownership changes afterward and eventually closed.

15.6 mi **Cleghorn Springs:** When D. B. Cleghorn and his family started a ranch at this location in 1878, the spring flowing into Rapid Creek took their name. Before then it was known as Big Springs. The combination of water and a wide meadow had long attracted people, from American Indians to early military expeditions to John Brennan and his associates, who spent a night here as they ventured down Rapid Creek in February 1876. One California Joe laid out a townsite that he called Upper Rapid in the foothills near Big Springs a week after Brennan's party established Rapid City, but California Joe's town failed to develop. Then the Cleghorns came along. When the Upper Rapid City Company built Canyon Lake in 1890, it also planned a small suburb near the springs. That development failed to prosper. The federal government eventually built a water pipeline from the springs to its Rapid City Indian School in 1908.

15.7 mi **Fish hatchery:** The state opened a small hatchery in Rapid City in 1916. As demand exceeded production, the state began purchasing trout from hatcheries in other states. To make up for the shortfall, the South Dakota Game and Fish Commission decided to build a new hatchery at Cleghorn Springs and purchased the springs in 1927. The location had what the commissioners wanted: a constant flow of ice-cold water. When the hatchery opened in early 1929, the state anticipated hatching and rearing two million trout to fingerling size per year. The hatchery was remodeled in the 1940s and again after the 1972 flood nearly destroyed it.

The Chapel in the Hills, seen in a postcard. Nestled in the hills five miles from Rapid City, it is a full-sized replica of the famous Borgund Stavkirke in Norway. *South Dakota State Historical Society*

16.0 mi **Chapel in the Hills:** One mile south on Chapel Lane is a replica of a Norwegian *stavkirke,* or stave church, built in 1969. Harry Gregerson, the originator of the Lutheran Vespers radio program, inspired its construction. He wanted a home for his radio ministry that would attract more followers and honor South Dakotans of Norwegian heritage. The radio show has since moved to Minneapolis, and a nonprofit corporation now welcomes visitors to the Chapel in the Hills. It was listed on the National Register of Historic Places in 2012.

16.2 mi **Canyon Lake:** Developers wished to dam Rapid Creek since Rapid City's earliest days, and the Upper Rapid City Company finally succeeded in 1890. Organized by Kentucky and Rapid City capitalists, including Valentine McGillycuddy, the company planned to build a small subdivision and a summer resort, with the lake as the centerpiece. The investors purchased nearly 1,000 acres of land, laid out streets, and planted "several thousand trees." They then hired C. D. Crouch to construct a log-and-earth-filled dam across Rapid Creek. The completed dam was wide enough to hold three carriages standing side by side. The company then built a boathouse, bought fifteen boats, and held a contest to name the new body of water. Canyon Lake beat out such suggestions as Lake Lucerne, the name of a lake in Switzerland. The new lake created plenty of interest, especially since the Black Hills had no natural lakes and only a few small dams at the time. As a local journalist claimed, Rapid City now had the one feature that the Black Hills had been sorely lacking.

The Upper Rapid City Company's next move was to build a large hotel and a trolley line to downtown Rapid City, about four miles away, but it ran out of money. Creating Canyon Lake was its only accomplishment. The Dakota Water Power Company bought the dam hoping to generate power in 1895, but that too failed to happen. As civic leaders debated how best to use Canyon Lake, Rapid City residents began using it as a recreational getaway. Tragedy struck in 1907 when a flood washed out the dam, killing four people. City voters, uninterested in rebuilding the dam, defeated a bond issue that would have underwritten the cost. Dr. Robert J. Jackson, who ran a nearby dairy farm, subsequently took control of the lakebed.

Some community leaders, envisioning the lake as a tourist attraction, still wanted the dam rebuilt, especially since Rapid City had recently opened a municipal tourist park in the vicinity. Their efforts finally paid off when the federal government provided the funds through the Reconstruction Finance Corporation (RFC) in 1932. Established by the federal government to provide financial support to state governments, banks, railroads, and other businesses impacted by the Depression, the RFC also served to create jobs. It funded construction at Legion Lake in Custer State Park and at Reausaw Lake on Hay Creek. Though often associated with the New Deal, these projects were started during the Hoover administration. In any case, the Black Hills benefitted from the infusion of federal dollars. The government provided between $20,000 and $25,000 for Canyon

Lake, while Dr. Jackson donated the land, with the stipulation that no motorboats would be permitted. The new dam was completed, and the lake filled in April 1933. As hoped, tourist businesses soon opened nearby, including "Nystrom's on Canyon Lake," which promoted sixteen "ultra-modern cottages," along with boating, fishing, and swimming. Another early business was the Canyon Lake Tavern. Started in 1933, it eventually became a night club known as the Canyon Lake Supper Club and operated until 1990.

The new Canyon Lake dam withstood periodic floods for thirty-nine years until the massive 1972 flood caused it to fail. Some witnesses state that the resulting surge of water greatly added to the loss of life and property—in all, the flood killed 238 people and caused $160 million in damage. Experts who have analyzed the flood, however, claim that the dam's failure had little overall impact. Because of the lake's aesthetic appeal, the city decided to rebuild. With input from the U.S. Army Corps of Engineers, the new dam was designed to mitigate any chance of failure. State and federal sources provided the $800,000 to rebuild it in 1976.

**Jackson Boulevard:** When the railroad through Rapid Canyon was abandoned, the city built a street over part of the right-of-way, naming it Jackson Boulevard after Dr. Robert J. Jackson in 1949. Besides donating the land for Canyon Lake, Jackson had also backed a residential development in the area and had served as the city's mayor.

**Garden Cottages Motel, 4030 Jackson Boulevard:** As auto travel boomed after World War II, entrepreneurs recognized Rapid City as the perfect place to build lodging. With US 14 and US 16 directing tourists through town, it had truly become the Gateway to the Black Hills. In 1953, Leland Case counted seventy-two tourist courts and three hotels in Rapid City. For the most part, these were independently owned and operated. The majority have disappeared. The Garden Cottages Motel is one of the last remaining examples.

17.0 mi **Meadowbrook Golf Course and the 1972 flood:** A nine-hole golf course and a housing subdivision once sat in the area on the right (south). The 1972 flood devastated the area. In the wake of that disaster, the city replaced the houses with an eighteen-hole golf course.

17.9 mi **At the intersection of Jackson Boulevard and Sheridan Lake Road, turn left (north) onto Sheridan Lake Road. Take Sheridan Lake Road to West Main Street.**

18.0 mi **Storybook Island, 1301 Sheridan Lake Road:** Inspired by Fairyland Park in Oakland, California, the Rapid City Rotary Club decided to construct and maintain a young people's playground known as Storybook Island in 1959. The backers of Oakland's Fairyland felt that traditional amusement parks offered little for young people beyond carousel rides and cotton candy. They wanted to offer something more kid-friendly and decided to recreate scenes from well-known nursery rhymes. Fairyland opened in 1948.

Rapid City's Storybook Island started out small, with twelve nursery rhyme scenes dispersed over two acres of land, but with the support of many people, the park slowly expanded. The 1972 flood washed away most of the figurines. Luckily many of them were recovered and restored. To better withstand future floods, the park was moved to higher ground a short distance from its original location. Several cities once hosted similar attractions, but most of these parks have disappeared. Rapid City's Storybook Island and a park in Aberdeen, South Dakota, are among the few that remain.

18.4 mi **Rapid City Indian Health Service, 3200 Canyon Lake Drive:** West of Sheridan Lake Road on Canyon Lake Drive is the Rapid City Indian Health Service Hospital. The federal government established the Rapid City Indian School at that location in 1898. Its mission was to assimilate American Indian children into white society. Government officials frequently had to coerce American Indian families to send their children to the school. Once enrolled, the students were taught English and manual trades, such as farming, and forbidden to practice their cultural traditions. Life in the school was often difficult, and several children died. The school lasted thirty-five years, with the enrollment topping three hundred during much of that time.

Sioux Sanatorium, later known as Sioux San Hospital, 1973. *Watson Parker Ghost Town Notebooks, Leland D. Case Library for Western Historical Studies, Black Hills State University*

Two factors seem to have led to its closing in the early 1930s: the government began questioning the boarding school model, and a tuberculosis outbreak raised concerns about disease among the students. The CCC, in conjunction with the WPA, converted the complex into a tuberculosis clinic for American Indians known as Sioux Sanatorium, or Sioux San for short. The Sanatorium opened in 1938 and lasted into the 1960s. The disease took a heavy toll, and many people were buried on the facility's grounds. As the need to treat tuberculosis diminished, the facility became part of the Indian Health Service.

When the federal government established the Indian school, it also set aside 1,200 acres of land where the students learned to raise crops and handle dairy cows. The products were consumed at the school, helping it to become self-sufficient. After the school's mission changed, the government turned much of the land over to Rapid City, which used it for schools and parks. Some people have argued that the land should have been set aside for the benefit of the American Indian population.

18.6 mi **Camp Rapid National Guard Headquarters:** The South Dakota National Guard began holding its summer encampments at what became known as Camp Rapid in 1924. The Guard had been meeting in Aberdeen, but it needed additional room for artillery practice. Camp Rapid, located two miles from Rapid City at the time, offered plenty of space. Once the initial encampment came to an end, Rapid City officials began promoting the site as a permanent home for the Guard. It took nearly a decade of lobbying, but the Guard eventually moved its operations to Camp Rapid. The WPA constructed a warehouse, a mess hall, a headquarters, and other buildings in 1934. Several other structures followed, including a sizable officers' mess. The Guard has constructed new buildings and altered several of the historic structures over the years. The native stone walls that surround the site are reminders of the WPA's work.

**Cement Plant:** In the distance, to the northwest, is the GCC Cement Plant. Progressive Republicans, led by Governor Peter Norbeck, felt that out-of-state businesses were treating South Dakota consumers unfairly in the 1920s. This led them to create several state-owned businesses, including a cement plant. The state chose Rapid City for the availability of local raw materials, including limestone, shale, and gypsum. Opening in 1925, the plant operated for seventy-five years as a state-owned enterprise. In 2000, the state sold it to GCC of America, a subsidiary of a large Mexican firm, for $252 million. Although the plant had been returning about $12 million a year to the state, Governor Janklow said that he took the action for "economic reasons." A governor's aide stated that the cement business had become more competitive, and the aide anticipated that the plant would begin losing money.

**Black Hawk:** A short distance north of the cement plant is the community of Black Hawk, named for a nearby creek. Historian Leland Case once wondered why a Black Hills location was named after a Sac and Fox chief from Illinois, especially with so many local American Indians to choose from. The most likely reason is that the creek and town were named after another Western town with the same name, such as Black Hawk, Colorado. This Black Hawk was established as the Fremont, Elkhorn & Missouri Valley Railroad built through in 1887. The town grew slowly, but as Rapid City prospered, Black Hawk became a bedroom community to its larger neighbor.

18.7 mi **At the intersection of Sheridan Lake Road and West Main Street, turn right onto Main Street.**

19.1 mi **Baken Park:** The large shopping center on the right (south) was built in the mid-1950s. It sits on land that was homesteaded in 1905 and then purchased by William P. Baken in 1920. The location was a little distance from downtown Rapid City, but Baken saw possibilities. With US 14 running where Main Street is today, and automobile travel on the rise, he opened a "tourist park," a store, and a dance pavilion, naming it "Baken Park." Sam Baldwin bought out Baken in 1925, but he kept the name as he expanded the business over the next twenty years. He eventually had eighty-two tourist cottages, with the Rapid City paper later calling it the largest and oldest motel in South Dakota. Baldwin sold the property to Stanton Neil in 1946, who sold it in turn to real estate developer Owen Mann in 1955. To make room for the shopping center, Mann moved several of the buildings farther west on US 14, where he opened "Owen Mann's Baken Park Motel."

20.0 mi **Return to Downtown Rapid City.**

## Conclusion

# From Gold Mining to Tourism

The Black Hills History Tours explore topics as varied as the discovery of gold, gold camps, town growth, mining companies, wagon roads, railroading, logging, American Indian relations, and tourism. Because the tours discuss history based on location, the "big picture" is often lost. Individual narratives can overwhelm a topic's larger historical significance or any connections that may exist between the different places. Many of the sites in fact experienced similar events, and by drawing these together, a fuller understanding of each topic can be uncovered. Gold towns and tourist attractions frequently come up in this tour and can be examined more deeply.

Every town this tour visits came into existence because of gold, but with some differences in why and when that happened. Prospectors established Custer, Hill City, Golden City (Sheridan), and Camp Crook (Pactola) near their placer claims in the first months of the Black Hills Gold Rush, hoping to create convenient service centers that would grow into permanent cities. At that same time, a group of prospectors led by John Brennan left their mountain claims to lay out a town on the edge of the Black Hills. Although the new town was established miles from the gold deposits, Rapid City's founders felt they had picked a location that would allow it to become a regional supply center, much as Denver had been for Colorado. About fifteen years later, hard rock miners located the town of Keystone next to the Keystone Mine. Regardless of their differences, towns that rely on gold often have uncertain futures. Most boom and bust, a pattern so common that historians have studied it. William Turrentine Jackson described it as a three-year cycle that begins with the discovery of gold, followed by a rush, and then a decline that ultimately results in the camp becoming a ghost town—although a ghost town might gain a new lease on life as a tourist attraction. All the towns in the Central Hills tour followed the boom-to-bust pattern, and most of them became ghost towns, at least for a time. Their ultimate fates, however, differed. Two disappeared entirely, three became tourist towns, and one grew into a major trade center. Understanding how that happened helps explain why some towns survive while others perish.

For Custer, Hill City, Sheridan, and Pactola, the bust came quickly. All of them roared to life as prospectors explored French, Spring, and Rapid Creeks in late 1875 and early 1876. These creeks, however, had only limited amounts of gold, and when the news of far richer deposits in Deadwood Gulch spread through the Black Hills, most miners left their claims, cabins, and towns to head north in the summer of 1876. Once there, a few fortunate miners struck it rich, while most found little. The less fortunate needed to find other ways to survive. Some of them returned to the central and southern Black Hills, where they reopened placer claims, searched for hard rock mines, or turned to other pursuits such as timbering and ranching, bringing Custer, Hill City, Sheridan, and Pactola back to life. The towns remained small. Only Custer had enough people (270) to be listed in the 1880 census, thanks in part to it becoming the Custer County seat in 1879. The three other camps were all but abandoned.

Periodic economic developments helped keep the four communities alive. For instance, the reported discovery of tin near today's Black Elk Peak brought the Harney Peak Tin Company into existence in 1883. The company purchased claims, dug shafts, and constructed several buildings in Hill City and Custer before collapsing in 1893. Although it recovered little tin, this activity brought a small boom, especially since it helped persuade the Burlington railroad to build through Hill City and Custer on its way to Deadwood in 1890. The rail connection made goods and markets more accessible, allowing entrepreneurs to open sawmills and exploit the area's pegmatite minerals, primarily mica and feldspar. By 1900, both towns had populations of around 600. Their earlier busts had apparently been put behind them.

Sustained economic prosperity proved elusive. The timber and mineral industries failed to sustain growth, and while Custer managed to maintain its population, Hill City again flirted with becoming a ghost town, especially after a fire destroyed much of the town in 1902. Custer and Hill City, however, survived and even began to thrive as tourism grew. They attracted tourists not because of their ghost town pasts, but because they were convenient stops on the way to Custer State Park,

Mount Rushmore, Crazy Horse Memorial, and the 1880 Train. Today, hundreds of thousands of people visit the two towns each year, but few know of their gold rush histories or how prospectors had founded them as gold camps.

If location helped Custer and Hill City survive, it did the opposite for Pactola and Sheridan. When these towns came back to life in the aftermath of the Deadwood Gulch excitement, miners, settlers, and promoters had high hopes for the gold camps. Changing the names from Camp Crook to Pactola and from Golden City to Sheridan reflected some of that optimism. Pactola's residents not only dreamed of a river of gold, as the name implies, but of untapped mineral riches throughout Rapid Canyon. The people behind Sheridan hoped town growth would bring profits, and they used their influence to have it named the seat of Pennington County and to have federal offices established there. But Pactola's mineral resources proved limited, and Sheridan soon lost the government offices. The towns survived by serving as way stations to nearby wagon roads. Despite their proximity to established trails, the Burlington bypassed Pactola and Sheridan when it built north in 1890. Sixteen years later, the Rapid Canyon Line built through Pactola, but it did little for the town except to make nearby timber resources more accessible to loggers. Similarly, Sheridan remained a small mountain outpost, even after the Warren-Lamb Lumber Company built its logging railroad along Spring Creek and past the town in the 1920s. Sheridan and Pactola eventually disappeared when the federal government built dams on Spring and Rapid Creeks, flooding the townsites. In an odd twist of fate, when government surveyors decided on these locations for the dams, they confirmed that the prospectors of 1876 had picked the most open and convenient spots to build.

Keystone was also founded on gold, albeit fifteen years after the gold rush and not because of placer gold. Instead, the discovery of hard rock gold veins led to the opening of the Keystone and Holy Terror Mines in the 1890s. The men who located the Keystone Mine also laid out the town. It boomed for the ten years that the mines operated. Once the gold mines closed, the town went bust, surviving despite several fires because of a rail connection and nearby pegmatite mines. President Calvin Coolidge's visit on his way to dedicate Mount Rushmore in 1927 demonstrated that the town's future lay in tourism. Over the next three decades, Keystone went from supplying the workers at Mount Rushmore to offering everything a tourist might want in "new" Keystone, built next to the old mining town. Much like Hill City and Custer, the gold town became a tourist town, not because of its history, but because of its location near Mount Rushmore.

Like the other towns, Rapid City was established by prospectors, but it sat the farthest from any gold finds. John Brennan and his associates left their Palmer Gulch claims to establish a "Denver of the Black Hills" in early 1876. Brennan knew well that location mattered. To create a gold rush service center, his town needed connections to trails and railroads, water for industries, space for growth, and agricultural lands nearby. Although technically not a gold camp, Rapid City still went through a boom-and-bust lifecycle. Within months of its founding, Rapid City nearly became a ghost town as Lakotas protested the intrusion on the Sioux Reservation and killed several settlers. Many residents fled, but Brennan and a handful of other brave souls refused to leave, building a blockhouse for protection. After the threat subsided, the inhabitants worked to ensure the town's growth. They opened trails, recruited businesses, and sought railroads. Despite some success, such as becoming the county seat, the town remained a remote outpost of the gold rush, best known for selling hay to passing bull teams. It was not until the Fremont, Elkhorn & Missouri Valley Railroad arrived in 1886, ten years after the town's founding, that it experienced a surge of growth and the community's future seemed secure.

Rapid City fell on hard times again when the Elkhorn built north to get closer to the mines in the northern Black Hills the very next year. To recover some of the town's lost vigor, local boosters sought another rail connection and underwrote the construction of several ore processing plants. None of these projects brought an economic boost. Three railroads finally did arrive in the early twentieth century, but with minimal influence from local promoters. The Chicago and North Western built in from Ft. Pierre and the Chicago, Milwaukee and St. Paul built from Chamberlain, expanding Rapid City's market reach to include much of western South Dakota. The Rapid Canyon Line to Mystic gave Rapid City a direct connection to the heart of the Black Hills. New industries followed, including a meat packing plant and what became known as the Warren-Lamb Lumber Company. The rail connections also allowed Rapid City to attract more tourists, especially as work on Mount Rushmore began and the Hotel Alex Johnson opened.

The Great Depression slowed the town's development, but with World War II came the predecessor of Ellsworth AFB. Postwar prosperity laid the groundwork for a vibrant economy. Through its ups and downs, Rapid City survived because of its location and because of the efforts of its founders. John Brennan's dream of Rapid City emulating Denver essentially came true. Just as Denver serves as the gateway to the Rocky Mountains, Brennan's town ultimately became the gateway to the Black Hills. To ensure Rapid City maintains this status, especially since tourism has become a key industry, city boosters have filled the downtown street corners with statues of presidents. By creating the "city of presidents," they have guaranteed that visitors will associate their town with Mount Rushmore.

Tourism is a vital industry to the central Black Hills in general. Outside the towns, the highways are dotted with roadside attractions, providing a wide variety of options for visitors to choose from. This diversity of offerings reflects, in part, how the business of tourism has changed over the years.

Black Hills tourism began when people saw the hot springs in the southern hills as a place to relax, enjoy the mountain environment, and restore their health. R. D. Jennings, Fred Evans, and their partners hoped to profit from this impulse when they claimed the mineral hot springs and created the town of Hot Springs in 1881. While stagecoaches were the primary means of transportation, visitor traffic was limited, but when railroads arrived in 1890–1891, patronage increased dramatically. Evans capitalized on the influx by opening Evans Plunge, a large swimming pool and bathing spa, and the Evans Hotel, a five-story, state-of-the-art lodging facility. The opening of Wind Cave just north of Hot Springs added to the town's appeal and helped make it a popular tourist destination.

Theodore Reder, a Black Hills sawmill owner, understood that the combination of an attractive setting and a railroad connection made a tourist destination possible. Soon after the Burlington railroad reached Custer in 1890, he created Sylvan Lake and built a hotel, hoping to attract long-term visitors. The location had just one drawback: it was seven miles from Custer and required a rough stagecoach ride to reach it.

Railroads gave Black Hills tourism its first big push, but the importance of rail travel was supplanted when automobiles arrived. If any one person deserves credit for introducing automobile tourism to the Black Hills, it would be Peter Norbeck. The South Dakota politician and two of his friends made the first auto trip across western South Dakota to the Black Hills in 1905. Once he saw the southern Black Hills, Norbeck believed it would be the perfect place to create a state game preserve. His efforts eventually led to the opening of Custer State Park in 1919. To make the park as appealing as possible, he made sure it included the Needles and Sylvan Lake, and to make it accessible he developed a highway through the Needles in 1921. In essence, Norbeck turned the rock spires into one of the Black Hills' first roadside attractions.

With the federal, state, and county governments working to improve roads, auto tourism and roadside attractions expanded throughout the 1920s. The increase in auto travel coincided with the fiftieth anniversary of the gold rush, and the Society of Black Hills Pioneers wanted to make sure it was not forgotten. In conjunction with Custer business clubs, the Pioneers erected the Gold Rush Monument in 1921, the Annie Tallent Monument in 1924, and rebuilt the Gordon Stockade in 1925. When a large crowd turned out for the dedication of the Gold Rush Monument, the Custer Women's Civic Club was inspired to sponsor an annual Gold Discovery Days pageant. Although these attractions were small compared to what would come later, they served the same purpose: to get travelers off the road and expose them to something out of the ordinary.

When South Dakota state historian Doane Robinson suggested carving figures from Western history in the Needles in 1923, he was essentially expanding on what Norbeck and the Society of Black Hills Pioneers had started. Robinson's notion of featuring such people as Red Cloud and Lewis and Clark, however, quickly disappeared once he persuaded Gutzon Borglum to do the work. Borglum had no small ideas and recognized his opportunity to do patriotic art on a grand scale. Not interested in a mere roadside attraction, he selected Mount Rushmore as the location and the nation's greatest presidents as his subjects, envisioning not just the presidential carvings, but developing an entablature and a hall of records that would highlight the nation's past and turn the site into a destination where people would spend time contemplating its meaning.

Borglum feared that roadside attractions would corrupt the monument's meaning. To help prevent that from happening, the park service included 1,300 acres of land as a buffer for the memorial. Still, Keystone quickly grew just outside of the boundaries. Its first tourist businesses catered to travelers' basic needs—gasoline and food—but as tourism increased, the shops began offering everything from souvenirs to educational opportunities. Despite the variety of businesses, Keystone's location in a narrow gulch limited what could be built. Several large roadside attractions opened along the highways between Rapid City and Mount Rushmore, where there was abundant space and ample tourist traffic.

Alex Duhamel opened one of the first of these roadside attractions on US 16 when he established Sitting Bull Crystal Caverns in 1934. By that time, six other Black Hills caves already offered tours, including two publicly owned caves, Wind and Jewel Caves. Despite the competition, Sitting Bull Caverns had three advantages: it was easily accessible; it had some of the largest crystals found in any local cave; and Duhamel moved his Sioux Indian Pageant there in 1936. He had offered this program of Indian dances and demonstrations at his Rapid City store, beginning in 1927. Duhamel further enhanced the show by building an octagonal dance hall, a tipi-shaped ticket office, and a trading post.

Other Rapid City businessmen, led by George Mansfield, wished to capitalize on the growing tourist traffic to invigorate Rapid City's economy. Their vision included building a scenic highway and opening roadside attractions along the ridge of what was known as Hangman's Hill, just west of downtown Rapid City. The city and its chamber of commerce persuaded the WPA to build Skyline Drive and five life-size dinosaurs for what became known as Dinosaur Park. Then the chamber decided to open Skyline Petrified Forest, featuring the petrified wood found on the hillside. With Skyline Drive offering access to panoramic views of Rapid City and the Black Hills, as well as to Dinosaur Park and the Petrified Forest, Mansfield and other town boosters felt they had created what would become a premier tourist destination.

Another Rapid City promoter, Earl Brockelsby, helped Rapid City's efforts when he opened Reptile Gardens in 1937. Brockelsby recognized that people were both terrified and fascinated by reptiles, and with rattlesnakes readily available in western South Dakota, he created a roadside attraction near the junction of Skyline Drive and US 16. Always aware of the importance of location and accessibility, Brockelsby became quite concerned when the highway department relocated US 16 a quarter mile east of his building. Although the change was not great, it still motivated him to move his attraction to a large tract of land in the Spring Creek basin in 1964. There he had good access to US 16 and the space to enlarge his business, which included adding a translucent dome where he could create a tropical forest and bring in a wider array of animals. In essence, Brockelsby had changed his business model. In the beginning, he and most other tourist promoters featured what the Black Hills had to offer, such as snakes, caves, or Native culture. When Brockelsby expanded his attraction, he relied much more on plants and animals that had no connection to the Black Hills but would appeal to visitors.

Once Mount Rushmore was completed and World War II ended, tourist travel increased dramatically. With the influx of people came entrepreneurs who opened more attractions that had little to do with the Black Hills' natural features. Instead, they were inspired by what they had seen elsewhere and believed would work in the Black Hills. The Cosmos Mystery Area is one example. A young man opened this attraction, claiming that he had found a location where "gravity faults" and "supernatural forces" existed. A similar gravity house had been established near his home in California, which undoubtedly inspired him to open the Cosmos. Two Rapid City businessmen also imported the idea of a marine animal show when they opened Marine Life. They knew the attraction had no connection to the Black Hills, but they also knew that people enjoyed marine shows and that there was not another one within one thousand miles. Then local dentist Doc Casey set up a drive-through wildlife park when he opened Bear Country. Bears once lived in the Black Hills, but none remained when Casey opened his attraction. Instead, he was inspired by a trip to Yellowstone, during which he saw how people responded to bears there.

Some of the more recent imports have been motivated by pop culture and amusement parks. For his movie *Dances with Wolves,* Kevin Costner constructed a small number of buildings to depict Fort Hays, Kansas, east of Rapid City. When he completed shooting, he left them behind and Herman Jones moved them to his property on US 16. After Jones opened them for tours, he added entertainment with the Chuckwagon Supper & Show. Since then, Jones has again expanded his attraction by opening the Buffalo Hunt Coaster ride. This amusement-park-style ride not only attracts more paying guests, but it also appeals to a new type of traveler who wants thrills and excitement while on vacation. As this implies, just as roadside attractions have changed, so have the tourists. At one time, visitors seemed satisfied to look at landscapes and natural features. Today, more and more tourists want to leave the merely picturesque behind and experience thrills and excitement.

# Bibliography

Developing tours that visit and discuss numerous locations and topics requires a wide variety of sources, but since the information is meant for a general audience, I have opted not to provide traditional endnote-style citations. Instead, this bibliography gives an overview of the most important sources I consulted and provides some direction as to where one might look to find more information about Black Hills history.

At least four publications already exist that can help a traveler navigate the region's past. In the 1930s, the Works Progress Administration hired unemployed writers to describe the history and culture of each state. The results of this effort, known as the Federal Writers' Project, include *A South Dakota Guide*. It comprises fifteen statewide tours, with the Black Hills mentioned in six. The South Dakota Guide Commission originally published the book in 1938, but it has since been republished, with the South Dakota Historical Society Press releasing a version in 2005. Leland D. Case, the noted western historian and benefactor to the Case Library for Western Historical Studies at Black Hills State University, published *Lee's Official Guidebook to the Black Hills and the Badlands* (1953). Although Case covered the region in just over one hundred pages, he still incorporated much interesting information, dedicating about one page to each of the larger communities. Finally, the "dean" of Black Hills history, Watson Parker, produced two useful books. For several years, Parker and his father, Troy, ran a guest ranch at Palmer Gulch, not far from Mount Rushmore. To help his guests navigate the region, Parker produced the *Palmer Gulch Lodge Guide to the Black Hills* (1960). More importantly, after countless hours locating and researching ghost towns, he and Hugh K. Lambert published *Black Hills Ghost Towns* (1974). The book lists and briefly describes around 600 locations, but because of the way it is organized, *Black Hills Ghost Towns* is difficult to use as a tour guide. Each listing includes a range, township, and section number, but since the towns are listed alphabetically, it is difficult to connect the locations. Moreover, all the publications mentioned above provide only limited information, and they are now quite dated.

For a person interested in learning more about Black Hills history in general, there are several books available. Luckily, many people who arrived with the gold rush wrote down what they saw and heard. Pioneer chronicles include Peter Rosen, *Pa-Ha-Sa-Pah: Or the Black Hills of South Dakota* (1895); Richard B. Hughes, *Pioneer Years in the Black Hills* (1957); John S. McClintock, *Pioneer Days in the Black Hills* (1939); Jesse Brown and A. M. Willard, *The Black Hills Trails* (1924); and Annie D. Tallent, *The Black Hills, or, The Last Hunting Ground of the Dakotahs* (1899). All of these provide valuable insights into Black Hills history, but each has a different focus. For instance, McClintock has seventy-one brief chapters, each covering a distinct topic, from murders to sawmills. While informative, this format makes it difficult to get a good overview of the region's history. Brown and Willard have excellent information on early violence, but the broader aspects of settlement are generally ignored. Tallent's book gives the best summary of early Black Hills history, and people who study the region frequently rely on her, but she includes some incorrect information, and she has been criticized for her insensitivity toward the American Indian population.

With the assistance of the above sources, several authors have produced good syntheses of Black Hills history, but only three will be mentioned. Watson Parker's *Gold in the Black Hills* (1966) is a must-read for anyone interested in the region's past. Parker not only covers the big events, such as the Custer Expedition and the discovery of gold, but he also discusses the creation of towns, Indigenous-white relations, mining camp violence, and more. The Parker book also has a good bibliography that Black Hills researchers will find useful. Another good synthesis is *Gold, Gals, Guns, Guts* (1976), edited by Bob Lee, with the assistance of Stan Lindstrom and Wynn Lindstrom. Although focused on the northern Black Hills, the book gives a good summary of that region's past and brings the story up to 1976. Finally, journalist Robert J. Casey wrote an engaging monograph emphasizing excitement, titled *The Black Hills and Their Incredible Characters* (1949). Casey, however, needs to be used carefully; he includes stories that he heard without double-checking them for accuracy.

If one desires more information on a specific subject, several publications exist. Four motifs frequently appear in this tour guide: military expeditions, transportation, mining, and town development. Of the military expeditions that visited the Black Hills, the Central Hills Tour mentions four: Lieutenant Warren's Army Corps of Topographical Engineers survey of 1857, the Custer Expedition of 1874, the Newton–Jenney geological survey of 1875, and General Crook's 1875 effort to remove trespassing miners. From 1973 to 1974, *South Dakota History*, the quarterly journal of the South Dakota State Historical Society, published five articles by James D. McLaird and Lesta V. Turchen titled "Exploring the Black Hills, 1855–1875: Reports of the Government Expeditions." These articles reprinted excerpts from the Warren through the Custer Expeditions. Since Crook's trip into the Black Hills in 1875 did not involve exploration, McLaird and Turchen did not cover it. Information on Crook in the Black Hills can be found in Paul Magid's *The Gray Fox: George Crook and the Indian Wars* (2015). More details about the Newton–Jenney Expedition are available in the journals of Colonel Richard Irving Dodge, who chronicled the adventure while leading the military column that escorted the scientists. Published accounts include Colonel Dodge's *The Black Hills* (1965) and Wayne R. Kime's *The Black Hills Journals of Colonel Richard Irving Dodge* (1996). Because of Custer's notoriety and the repercussions of his 1874 Black Hills expedition, several books mention him and his trip. The most thorough account is Ernest Grafe and Paul Horsted, *Exploring with Custer: The 1874 Black Hills Expedition* (2002, revised 2023). A much smaller but still valuable look at the expedition is Donald Jackson's *Custer's Gold: The United States Cavalry Expedition of 1874* (1966).

Transportation, including wagons and railroads, was important to the development of the Black Hills. The first significant gold rush trail came out of Cheyenne. Agnes Wright Spring's *The Cheyenne and Black Hills Stage and Express Routes* (1948) provides much information about early stagecoach operations. Other trails soon developed, and local historians have produced works for nearly every one, such as Vernon S. Holst's *A Study of the 1876 Bismarck to Deadwood Trail* (1983) and Jan Cerney's *The Fort Pierre-Deadwood Gold Trail* (2006). A few studies give overviews of the trails, including Hyman Palais's "A Study of the Trails to the Black Hills Gold Fields," in *South Dakota Historical Col-*

*lections*, XXV (1951), and Irma H. Klock's *All Roads Lead to Deadwood* (1979). More information about trails and stagecoach operations can be found by visiting relevant websites. For instance, the Wyoming State Preservation Office has a site titled the "Cheyenne-Black Hills Stage Route Historic District," (wyoshpo.wyo.gov). Two authors provide thorough overviews of the construction and operation of Black Hills' rail lines. Mildred Fielder published "Railroads of the Black Hills" in *South Dakota Historical Collections*, XXX (1960), which she turned into a book, with many more photographs, in 1964. Railroad historian Rick Mills has written about South Dakota railroads in general, and he focused on the Black Hills in at least two publications. His most detailed effort is *125 Years of Black Hills Railroading* (2004).

Several sources are useful in learning about the region's mining past. Contemporaneous newspapers are invaluable. Since much of the region's economy depended on mining, newspapers often covered mining developments in detail. The most useful papers include Deadwood's *Black Hills Daily Times* and *Black Hills Pioneer*, although every Black Hills paper carried mining news, and most of them are available online. Several organizations, such as railroads, published books and brochures that promoted mining investments. One of the most useful came from the Black Hills Mining Men's Association, titled *The Black Hills Illustrated* (1904). Its intent was to encourage investment in underdeveloped mines, but it also contains much good information about the Black Hills in general. The South Dakota School of Mines was another source of mining news. For a time, it produced a regular publication that highlighted mining, although it also carried other Black Hills stories. It went by three names over the years: the *Aurum*, the *PaHaSaPa Quarterly*, and the *Black Hills Engineer*. On a national level, the *Engineering and Mining Journal* regularly carried Black Hills mining news and occasionally ran feature stories. Since the days of the 1857 Warren Expedition, the federal government has taken an interest in the Black Hills' mineral wealth, and that has continued through the years, resulting in publications that are helpful when exploring mining history. In particular, the Bureau of Mines produced two invaluable pieces. One is the *Black Hills Mineral Atlas, Part 1 and Part 2* (1954). These volumes list and briefly discuss every mine and mineral deposit that has been explored, developed, or located. They are a good starting point for understanding the extent and variety of mining activities. The other Bureau of Mines publication is Paul T. Allsman's *Reconnaissance of Gold-Mining Districts in the Black Hills, S. Dak.* (1940). While not as comprehensive as the *Mineral Atlas,* it provides more detailed information on the important mining companies.

The Central Hills Tour visits four towns (Rapid City, Keystone, Custer, and Hill City) and this bibliography focuses on resources related to those locations. Since Rapid City is the Black Hills' largest and arguably most important town, several fine publications have been written about its development. Ross P. Korsgaard examines the town's early history in "A History of Rapid City, South Dakota, During Territorial Days," in *South Dakota Historical Collections* 38 (1976). David B. Miller provides a fairly brief but well-done overview in *Gateway to the Hills: An Illustrated History of Rapid City* (1985). Longtime Rapid City resident, teacher, and historian David F. Strain delves much deeper in *Black Hills Hay Camp: Images and Perspectives of Early Rapid City* (1989, 2010). Along with excellent images, Strain includes maps that place historic businesses within the context of the modern city. While these publications greatly help in understanding the town's growth, two sources demonstrate how its architectural features changed over time: Adrienne Merola Kerst, Jean Oleson-Kessloff, and Patrick D. Roseland's *Rapid City: Historic Downtown Architecture* (2007), published as part of Arcadia Publishing's Images of America series; and the National Register of Historic Places listing of the Rapid City Commercial Historic District. Finally, the *Rapid City Journal* is an invaluable resource when exploring any topic related to the city and the surrounding region.

Published information about Custer, Hill City, and Keystone is more limited, but several sources contain good information. Fred W. Whitley's "A History of Custer City, South Dakota, 1874–1900," in *South Dakota Historical Collections* 37 (1975) looks at the first quarter century of the Black Hills' first town. Alice Davis Smith records some of Hill City's adventures in *Lowdown on Hilltown: Historical Annals of Hill City, South Dakota* (2002), and Martha Linde discusses seven central Black Hills towns in *Rushmore's Golden Valleys* (1976). Besides this published material, some communities provide good local histories via websites and walking tours. Keystone, for example, provides the "Historic Keystone Walking Tour." These towns also have historic buildings listed on the National Register of Historic Places, and the nomination forms often provide good information. An online search can help identify properties listed on the register, and the South Dakota State Historic Preservation Office (SHPO) in Pierre may be helpful. A good source on just about every Black Hills location is the Watson Parker Ghost Town Notebooks collection, located at the Leland D. Case Library for Western Historical Studies at Black Hills State University in Spearfish. These notebooks contain the research that Parker gathered over a lifetime and then summarized in *Black Hills Ghost Towns*. Another source that should not be ignored is *South Dakota Magazine*. This popular periodical occasionally highlights a Black Hills community.

The Central Hills Tour discusses several tourist attractions, with Mount Rushmore being the most prominent. Keeping with its stature, the monument's history is explored in several quality books. Gilbert Fite's *Mount Rushmore* (1952) took the first comprehensive look at the origin and development of the project. Rex Allen Smith followed up from a slightly different angle when he focused on the workers in *The Carving of Mount Rushmore* (1985). John Taliaferro focuses more on Gutzon Borglum, the monument's sculptor, in *Great White Fathers: The Story of the Obsessive Quest to Create Mount Rushmore* (2002). In recent years, Crazy Horse Memorial has become almost as famous and popular as Mount Rushmore, but it has yet to attract much literary attention. Of the existing publications, two were done by memorial employee Robb DeWall: *Korczak: Storyteller in Stone* (1984) and *Crazy Horse and Korczak* (1982). The memorial's quarterly newsletter, *Progress*, can also be informative. Reptile Gardens and Bear Country U.S.A., the two most popular interactive attractions, are discussed in books written about their founders. Don Theye looks at the man who started Bear Country in *Bear With Me: Dennis "Doc" Casey* (2002), while Sam Hurst examines the life of the founder of Reptile Gardens in *Rattlesnake Under His Hat: The Life & Times of Earl Brockelsby* (2016). Finally, a brief overview of tourist attractions can be found in David A. Wolff's "On the Road to Mt. Rushmore: The Changing Business of Tourism," in *The Black Hills Historian* (Fall 2023), produced by BHSU's Leland D. Case Library for Western Historical Studies.

In closing, there are many locations a researcher can find information, and perhaps the easiest place to start is online. The U.S. Forest Service, local businesses, tourist attractions, South Dakota Public Broadcasting, and outdoor recreation groups have websites that can provide good introductions to a topic or location. A web search may also identify relevant articles that have appeared in scholarly journals, such as *South Dakota History*. In total, there are many possible sources, and in putting this tour together, I checked most of them.

# Index